FULL
DISCLOSURE

Do You Really Want
to Be a Lawyer?

About the Illustrators

Michael L. Goodman clerked for Chief Judge James C. Turk in the U.S. District Court for the Western District of Virginia and is now a partner at Browder, Russell, Morris & Butcher in Richmond, Virginia, specializing in medical malpractice defense litigation. He is also an "Attorney-at-Draw" whose achievements include a comic strip called "Wingtips" and publications in the *Washington Post, Richmond Times-Dispatch, Legal Times,* and other national legal news publications.

Sam Hurt graduated from the University of Texas School of Law in 1983, practiced briefly, and is now a professional cartoonist in Austin, Texas. His primary cartoon character is Eyebeam, whose antics began in a university newspaper comic strip and now fill several books.

FULL DISCLOSURE

Do You Really Want to Be a Lawyer?

Compiled by Susan J. Bell
for the Young Lawyers Division
of the American Bar Association

Peterson's Guides

Princeton, New Jersey

Illustrations on pages 10 and 73 originally published by New Stream Comics, Austin, Texas, © 1986 and 1988, respectively, by Sam Hurt, reprinted with permission of the artist. Illustrations on pages 14 and 110 reprinted from *The Mind's Eyebeam,* published by Andrews & McMeel, © 1986 by Sam Hurt, with permission of the artist. Illustrations on pages 15, 16, 25, 30, 69, and 93 reprinted from *I'm Pretty Sure I've Got My Death-Ray in Here Somewhere!,* Andrews & McMeel, © 1982 by Sam Hurt, with permission of the artist. Illustrations on pages 20, 23, and 128 reprinted from *Eyebeam, Therefore I Am,* Andrews & McMeel, © 1984 by Sam Hurt, with permission of the artist. Illustration on page 63 reprinted from *Eyebeam: Teetering on the Blink,* published by Texas Monthly Press, © 1986 by Sam Hurt, with permission of the artist. Illustrations on pages 97, 103, and 164 reprinted from *Our Eyebeams Twisted,* Andrews & McMeel, © 1985 by Sam Hurt, with permission of the artist. Illustrations on pages 117, 152, and 158 reprinted from *Eenie Meenie Minie Tweed,* Andrews & McMeel, © 1985 by Sam Hurt, with permission of the artist. Illustration on page 125, © 1981 by Universal Press Syndicate, reprinted with permission of Michael L. Goodman.

Library of Congress Cataloging-in-Publication Data

Full disclosure : do you really want to be a lawyer? / compiled by Susan J. Bell for the Young Lawyers Division of the American Bar Association.
    p.   cm.
   ISBN 0-87866-867-5
   1. Practice of law—United States. 2. Law—Study and teaching—United States. I. Bell, Susan J., 1955– . II. American Bar Association. Young Lawyers Division.
KF300.F85   1989
340'.07'1173—dc19

88-36853
CIP

Composition and design by Peterson's Guides
Cover illustration by Michael L. Goodman
Illustrations by Michael L. Goodman and Sam Hurt

Printed in the United States of America

10 9 8 7 6 5 4 3 2 1

CONTENTS

PREFACE

You are contemplating a course of action that will change your life—the way you think, the way you plan, the way you live. Before you "cross the Rubicon," we would like you to know what's on the other side.

The Pre-Law Counseling Committee of the Young Lawyers Division of the American Bar Association undertook a two-year project beginning in August 1987 to write, edit, and publish a book to provide guidance to would-be lawyers about law school and the legal profession. This is an effort to give you who are considering joining our ranks the inside scoop—everything we wish we had known before we went to law school.

Twenty-four authors from across the country were enlisted to write chapters about aspects of the professional experience that will help you understand the world of being a lawyer. They represent a broad array of viewpoints to ensure that we provide you with a balanced, thorough, accurate view of law school and the legal profession.

Now, the "thank you's." My deepest appreciation to my team of hard-working, fun-loving final editors, Carolyn Ahrens, Rick Jenney, Margaret Price, and Cathy Reynolds, who revised each of the chapters in the book, turned a collage of individual works into a coherent whole, and sustained me on the days when I thought this project would never see the bookstore shelves.

Special thanks to William C. Hubbard and Christopher L. Griffin, the YLD chairs in 1987–88 and 1988–89, respectively, who were willing to take a risk on this scheme and provided the moral and financial support for the book. Hats off to all the Pre-Law Counseling Committee members who reviewed chapters and assisted in publicizing the book.

A special award of gratitude to Claudette Tremback, my secretary during 1987–88, who served more as my clone and made a special contribution to the book's success, and to Robin Lillicotch and the rest of the word processing staff in the Washington, D.C., office of Paul, Hastings,

Janofsky & Walker for their patience and talent through the book's many revisions.

    Finally, my heartfelt thanks to the authors and illustrators who enthusiastically responded to the idea of creating this book and diligently worked to share their experiences with you. All this so that you, would-be lawyers, can make an informed choice about joining the legal profession. Let your journey begin!

Susan J. Bell

Pre-Law Counseling Committee
1987–89

Chair
Susan J. Bell

Final Editors

Carolyn Ahrens	Margaret C. Price
Frederick E. Jenney	Cathy A. Reynolds

Primary Editors

Bradley J. Catt	David S. Goldstein
Herbert A. Claiborne III	Bradley Harrold
Leonard R. Cleavelin	Keith B. Norman
Valda Combs-Jordan	Joseph M. Weiler

Committee Members

John C. Brzustowicz	Archie C. Lamb Jr.
Carlos M. Chavez	Stacy E. Sallee
Todd Irwin Glass	Jeffrey L. Swartz

INTRODUCTION

With the publication of this book, the Young Lawyers Division of the American Bar Association takes a significant step forward in its efforts to enhance the quality of the legal profession and the opportunities it provides for all of its members. The various chapters will give each reader an honest and straightforward, yet sometimes humorous, view of the practice of law. Such a view can only allow for better-informed, and therefore more reliable, decisions about whether to enter law school and become a lawyer.

The Young Lawyers Division has as one of its primary goals the promotion of values that make lawyering a "different" profession. It does this out of an overriding concern for the future of the profession and the special place it holds in American society. That special place is a privilege, and one that has to be continually earned by each new generation of lawyers.

Lawyers are given an exclusive license to participate in our nation's administration of justice. With that license comes a concomitant obligation *to serve the public interest.* That service may be performed in many ways, from representing poor persons in routine civil disputes to giving free advice to victims of natural disasters, from participating in established legal aid clinics to providing assistance to the elderly in obtaining public health benefits, and also in devoting time to the service of the organized bar. The method, however, of a lawyer's public service is not as important as the service itself. All lawyers in this country *must,* as an indispensable part of professional life, use their education and skills for the public good in return for the privilege of being a lawyer. It is only by understanding that aspect of the practice of law that individuals can enter law school—and then the profession—fully aware of their obligation to their communities, people in need, and the American system of justice.

The subjects addressed in the following pages will allow each reader to better understand what being a lawyer is all about. You will learn about what goes on inside a law school and what lawyers really do after they leave law school. You will learn how people actually become lawyers and how they view different legal careers once they are lawyers. Each of these considerations is critical to an intelligent decision about your future.

It is our intention that those who read this book and who use it in deciding whether to enter the profession will do so knowing that it is a profession and not just a business. The law is a high calling, and we hope that those of you who are ready to contribute to the public good, adhere to the highest ethical standards, and promote the best interests in our system of justice will consider the law as your career.

William C. Hubbard
1987–88 Chairperson
Young Lawyers Division
American Bar Association

Christopher L. Griffin
1988–89 Chairperson
Young Lawyers Division
American Bar Association

PRACTICE
PRELIMINARIES

DO YOU REALLY WANT TO BE A LAWYER?

Susan J. Bell

Before you quickly retort "of course," take a few minutes to explore what being a lawyer is—and is not. Many of you will find another career after reading this book. Some of you will leave law school without Juris Doctor degrees. Of those who do finish, a surprising number will leave practice within five years. Some will practice law for many years—and enjoy it.

Prospective law students cite many reasons for wanting to be lawyers: to bring about social change, to assist others in need, for intellectual stimulation, for financial rewards, and for professional prestige. Can practicing law satisfy those desires? And at what price?

Law school provides three years of intellectual stimulation, of analyzing legal doctrines and learning to think critically. The adage goes, "If you like law school, you'll hate practice."

Practice certainly does not have to be devoid of intellectual pursuit. Some practices exist to solve the tough problems. Even the most routine practices include an occasional novel question that requires some extra research and thought to resolve.

Every practice, however, no matter how stimulating, has its fair share of repetitious, unexciting "scut" work. Reviewing tens of thousands of pages of corporate documents in cramped quarters in a city that's not in any travel agent's brochures is enough to dampen any young attorney's enthusiasm. After you've written a few discovery motions or completed some commercial transaction forms, you can do either when you're practically asleep.

Sleep is a commodity you may find in short supply as a practicing attorney. No matter what practice opportunity you choose, the hours are

Susan J. Bell practices litigation in Washington, D.C., and chaired the Pre-Law Counseling Committee of the ABA's Young Lawyers Division from 1987 to 1989 to create and publish this book. She is also the author of "Interviewing for Success and Satisfaction," a guide for law students published by the YLD, and she conducts career counseling programs for bar associations and individual lawyers.

likely to be long and unpredictable. In almost any position, you can expect to work some nights and weekends. In some practices you can expect to work many of them. You may find yourself out of town for weeks on end reviewing documents, taking depositions, trying a case, or working on a corporate acquisition. Canceled dates, unused tickets, and rescheduled vacations are a way of life.

Private law firms monitor how much sleep you've lost with billable hours recorded on time sheets. This is the amount of time you spend working on client projects, generally including the time you spend traveling to and from a destination, recorded on forms that request the client's name, an accounting code number, a description of your activity, and the amount of time you worked. Not every minute you spend in the office is billable. Administrative tasks such as reading professional material, interviewing attorneys who might be added to your staff, and completing travel vouchers and time sheets are charged to nonbillable accounts; no client pays the firm for your time spent on these tasks. As a general rule, 10 hours in the office will yield about 8 billable hours. Firms routinely require attorneys to bill 1,800 hours per year (and the number is rising). In fact, many attorneys bill closer to 2,000 or more.

Attorneys not in private practice obviously do not have to bill clients for their time. Many groups, however, still require a similar record-keeping system to monitor the amount of time each project receives.

Billable hours form the basis for the financial rewards that lure some students to the law. For the most talented and hardworking in America's major metropolitan areas, those rewards can be enormous. Associate attorneys fresh from law school were paid $70,000 a year in 1987 by New York's largest and most prestigious firms. Similar firms in other cities where living costs are less expensive offered as much as $58,000. Partners in the country's most lucrative firms draw from $300,000 to $500,000 a year, sometimes more.

The national averages paint a different picture. The median salary for beginning associates in 1988 was $36,000 and the average about $37,000, according to an August 1988 *ABA Journal* article. Those figures include firms of all sizes in all parts of the country.

Salaries among practice opportunities vary widely. Corporations and trade associations come closest to the salaries paid by large firms, but the gap is still large. Government salaries are next, with the federal government generally paying more than state or local governments. Salaries paid by public interest and legal services groups are usually lower than those paid to attorneys working in other organizations.

Legal positions outside private practice offer lower salaries but advertise other advantages—more responsibility earlier in your career, an opportunity to advocate socially useful actions or "do the right thing," and sometimes regular, reasonable hours. Associates practicing in a law firm for three years may be drafting motions and documents and may even argue motions in small state court cases or negotiate small deals. Their counterparts in government or public interest are likely to have primary responsibility for twenty or more cases. Briefs may be reviewed by two or three attorneys before they are filed, and supervising attorneys remain available for strategy discussions and questions.

"Doing the right thing" to effect social change is like eating an elephant—it's accomplished one bite at a time! Your "bites" as a young attorney will probably be individual cases in which you prosecute one criminal or fight one landlord. Sometimes you'll nail an entire drug ring or a major source of pollution or the owner of a large low-rent apartment building. You may even be the head of an agency, an attorney general, or a Supreme Court justice one day. At any level, you still have the satisfaction of working for your own political or social ideals.

You will probably find, however, that you accomplish any social change despite all odds. Your corporate opponents represented by large firms will generally have a myriad of resources unavailable to you, including more attorneys, paralegals, sophisticated computer equipment, and more able secretarial and support staff. You'll find yourself typing some of your own letters and memos and sometimes even your own briefs.

Every practice opportunity offers some kind of psychic satisfaction whether or not it effects social change. Large corporations have some unique problems that receive national attention, and they are willing to spend much money to have the problems solved. If you work in a large law firm, you enjoy the ability (and sometimes suffer the mandate!) to thoroughly explore every aspect of the company's legal woes and read about it in the morning paper. Corporations are also made of "human stuff," and some of those managers from the conglomerates that large law firms represent will become friends. That human element is even more apparent in practices that represent individuals and small businesses.

You may also enjoy developing your own clients and winning their trust and loyalty. Many of them will seek your advice on a myriad of legal issues and sometimes on business decisions. You may have the opportunity to assist a fledgling new business as it grows, help reinstate an employee, or save a corporate officer from facing criminal charges. A client's warm thanks for a job well done can sustain you through some of the tedium.

For those of you who are attracted to the profession's prestige, I have good news and bad news. Everyone will tell you that your studying law is an ambitious, laudable undertaking. A curious transition occurs in that attitude once you have passed the bar and begun practice. Suddenly you become a crook and shyster in the best Watergate and Iran-contra tradition.

Those scandals and the profession's transition to a business have contributed to lawyers ranking among groups Americans most distrust. Lawyers' legal (and sometimes illicit) antics make national headlines and the 6 o'clock news.

Practicing lawyers, especially litigators, need not rely on the media, however, to experience the profession's less-than-sterling element. Within the first five practice years, most lawyers will encounter an ally or an opponent whose work is shoddy or whose conduct is unethical. Such behavior is not limited to any particular firm size or substantive practice area.

© 1986 by Sam Hurt

And now, the good news. Only a few bad apples spoil the barrel of the profession. As I meet and work with other young lawyers nationwide, I am constantly amazed by their competence, enthusiasm, and dedication. They frequently volunteer much time and energy to public service activities after having already committed many hours to client matters.

Clients are the mainstay of the legal business; they are your customers and more. They come in many different forms—from federal and state agencies to the public at large, from multinational corporations to the corner bar, from well-established families to resident aliens. They provide some of the most rewarding and the most frustrating moments the profession offers. They mirror the general population. Some of them will be the most charming, reasonable folks you could ever hope to meet; others will be so distasteful that you and your colleagues will draw straws to determine who has to return their calls. Some of them will follow your advice; some of them will refuse it and blame you for the resulting problems. Some of them will ask you to make judgments based on factors only they can adequately weigh. When a case result is unfair, you will find yourself trying to explain and defend the entire legal system.

Clients are also the source of one of the profession's most often heard criticisms—that lawyers are just "hired guns." We advocate any position, within certain ethical bounds, that a client requests as long as we are paid. We represent the innocent and the guilty, the virtuous and the viceful, without a thought for doing justice. The response to that criticism is simple—justice is best served when all views are clearly and intelligently articulated—but you will have to use that response often.

Underlying the profession's hired gun aspect is another factor to consider before entering the profession: its reactive nature. With few exceptions, lawyers react and respond; they do not seek and create. They react to clients' requests to execute a building's purchase, to be compensated for injuries, to keep them out of jail, to defend them against another's erroneous actions. Lawyers do not choose what wrongs to right; they just represent individual clients' interests.

This can be a deeply rewarding profession that can assist you in fulfilling some of your goals. Just remember—the law is a jealous mistress. Do not underestimate what price the profession will demand.

STEP UP TO THE BAR
Surviving Law School

Carolyn Ahrens

Law school isn't as much fun as a picnic, but, as the author of this chapter points out, it can be to a large extent what you make it. Attorney Carolyn Ahrens shares a personal and humorous perspective on the challenges and ordeals of three years spent in law school.

There is a saying about the law school experience that goes something like this:

The first year of law school scares you to death;
The second year of law school works you to death; and
The third year of law school bores you to death!

These words have been passed down from law school class to law school class across the nation, although no one I talked to is aware of their origin. I heard it at the University of Texas School of Law.

To be repeated so often, the saying must have a great deal of truth in it; nevertheless, there is more to the story. I made it through law school, and I actually enjoyed it. Your law school experience, to a large extent, is what you make of it. Each year in the usual three-year law degree program is distinctly different. To survive law school, take one year at a time.

First Year
(What was so great about Socrates anyway?)

Law school begins with a formal orientation in which the administration and faculty thank you for your money, tell you what they are going to do

---

Carolyn Ahrens is an associate at the law firm of Booth & Newsom, P.C., in Austin, Texas, and serves on the Board of Directors of the Austin Young Lawyers Association and as Chairperson of the AYLA Law Student Division Committee. She gives many thanks to Michael Jewell, Austin Young Lawyers Association Law Student Liaison, for his help and insight.

to you for the next three years, and then try to comfort you. You can learn a great deal about your law school's philosophy at orientation, as well as learning the fundamentals of student life. The differences in school philosophies are significant.

At orientation, you may hear that only the best and brightest made it through the admissions process, so that every new student is expected to graduate. Or you may hear that one out of every three or four students will flunk out after the first year, and even more after the second year. While one school may emphasize teaching practical legal skills, another may emphasize legal theory. My alma mater told me at orientation that by the end of my three years I would have been taught to "think like a lawyer." Whether intended or not, orientation can scare you to death.

© 1986 by Sam Hurt

Depending on the size of the school you attend, you may see 600 or more fellow first-year law students at orientation. Although my law school background is limited to one university, informal research leads me to believe that certain experiences are common from place to place. My entering class was split into sections of 120 students each. Each section took all of its classes together for the first year. Each section was split further into mentor groups, called "TQ" groups after Teaching Quizmasters who led them. Teaching Quizmasters are third-year law students who teach oral advocacy and legal research and writing on a basis that is more informal than regular classes. Their duties include helping their first-year students to keep things in perspective. My group's TQ was known to us as "Dad."

The people you take classes with are the people whose faces you will come to know very well. They will share the pressures as well as the momentary reliefs with you for one very long year. Even at a school where the first-year environment is not competitive, you will realize that the people in your classes are the people whose grades will be computed on a bell curve right along with yours. Some of these people will be your best friends or your study companions. All of them will be with you at the bookstore trying to make essential purchases at the same time.

Forget those happy undergraduate days when you sauntered into classes on the first day of any given semester to hear the teachers introduce themselves, ask if this was really the class you intended to take, and tell you that you would meet at the same time next week for the first lecture. Law school first-year course schedules are prearranged, generally consisting of property law, torts, contract law, civil procedure, and constitutional law or some other configuration of those basics. Assignments have been posted or mailed out ahead of time. You are expected to have completed your assignment before the first class and to be ready to learn.

Many attorneys remember their first law school class very clearly. I remember crowding in to find my name on an alphabetical seating chart, locating my chair, and then waiting. I was waiting for the very severe Professor Kingsfield character from "The Paper Chase" reruns on television to appear. Instead, in walked a young man wearing corduroy shorts and Topsiders who introduced himself as the teacher. Professor Kingsfield taught my second class.

The textbooks used by first-year-course professors are a compilation of written opinions rendered by courts in actual cases, with a little bit of explanation to tie the cases together. Clear-cut rules of law in the subjects studied are seldom revealed, if they even exist. Knowledge comes from studying old rulings as well as new, from studying cases decided on conflicting theories of law, and even from studying opinions that have been overruled. Legal theories begin to surface only after reading many such cases. In some classes, comprehensible rules will appear only at the end of the semester, if at all.

© 1982 by Sam Hurt

You prepare for classes by reading the cases that will be covered by the professor the next day and "briefing" them. When you brief a case, you summarize the pertinent facts, <u>identify the primary legal questions in-volved</u> and the <u>court's ruling,</u> and <u>outline the major legal points</u> the court considered in making its decision. Some students outline their case briefs, while others prefer to "book brief" by making notes in their texts. Briefs are not turned in to your professor for grading; you do them to brace for the inevitable—being called on in class.

Ask second-year law students what it was about the first year that un-nerved them, and their answer will likely include being called on in class to explain a case or to answer questions. A popular method of legal in-struction takes its name from the ancient Greek philosopher and teacher Socrates. A teacher using the Socratic method poses problems rather than giving solutions and asks questions rather than lecturing.

I was given two bits of advice for my first year: to keep my mouth shut and invest in my future by buying the best course outline I could afford. The advice about keeping my mouth shut seemed pretty good; however, except for a few people who quickly earned reputations as "gunners," everyone else must have gotten the same tip. When no one volunteers, professors will call on someone to answer their inquiries. Even if a stu-dent does volunteer, professors will ask someone else to agree or dis-agree and to explain why. Some professors do not like volunteers, prefer-ring to examine the expressions of the students and to call the name that matches the most apprehensive among them. Being on the receiving end of Socratic inquiry is like playing a game you just can't win. Even if you have an answer, follow-up questions will get you every time. Profes-sors have been doing this for years, giving them a decidedly unfair advan-tage. It helps to remember that almost every student in the room feels the same way you do.

© *1982 by Sam Hurt*

One of the few things worse than being called on in class is being called on when you are unprepared. The embarrassment is easier to get over than the way your grades may suffer. In one class, my professor allowed three unprepared days, except that to enjoy such protection you had to turn in your written "pass" before class started. If you turned in your pass, he would not call on you. If he called on you and you were unprepared but had not turned in a pass, it meant automatic points off your final grade. Skipping class when you have not studied usually won't help, because missed classes can also mean lost points.

Preparation, preparation, and more preparation is what first-year law academia is all about. Preparing for class ultimately is preparing for exams. This is when an outline becomes important. Although easier said than done, it's a good idea to keep exam preparation in mind throughout the year and to develop an outline as you go. A commercial course outline can help you bring together the concepts you will be given in bits and pieces by those professors who take Socrates too seriously, but commercial outlines cannot replace your own hard work and should be used more like a security blanket. Synthesize your class notes and the cases you studied and incorporate these into the commercial outlines. The act of creating your own outline is as helpful as the finished product when exam time comes. A personal computer is very handy for composing outlines, as well as for doing research papers. Some students find that forming study groups early in the year allows them to share the outlining burden and makes preparing for classes more enjoyable. For others, the group approach may be a waste of time.

Despite what you have read so far, pressure, hard work, and tedium need not overtake your life. Continuing to hold a job during the first year of law school only adds to this problem and is generally not a good idea. Maintaining other familiar activities, particularly if those activities include a marriage and a family, however, *is* a good idea. There is no doubt that law school puts a strain on personal relationships. As they say, forewarned is forearmed. An associate of mine who was married during law school offered the following bit of wisdom. When you go through school with a family, your studies must become a family effort or you may find yourself increasingly isolated.

There is also a law school social scene that helps ease the tension. Your class or section will likely organize a party or two. You may find that those in your mentor group, or in my case the TQ group, become happy-hour companions. There are law school fraternities and other student associations organized on most campuses. There are local bar association affiliates and student governments. Then there are the all-campus activities. During my first year at the University of Texas, we had a Halloween party, a "Spring Fling" barbecue and dance, a law week, intramural sports competitions, and a theatrical production called "Assault and Flattery" in which students and faculty members parodied themselves and each other. The somewhat underground Kamikaze Law Student Association also held a party with the student spoof law firm of Saliva and Sloth, P.C. Now that was a bash. However, back to the pressure, hard work, and tedium.

"First-year exams." Even now, those words can send a shudder up the spine of any attorney who has not been able to block out the memory. Although some schools have finals after each semester, all except one of my first-year final exams were in the spring and covered a year's worth of material. Midterm grades control only a small percentage of the final grade.

Imagine this. You worked as diligently as you could all year, but your outlines are just two thirds done, and yes, there are some cases you have not read. Exams are spread over several weeks, and you hope you still have time to get everything done. You go into seclusion and begin a study frenzy—thinking law, breathing law, even sleeping law—for days and nights on end. Then the time comes for your first exam. You pull on your lucky tennis shoes, pack your lucky pens, and reread your outline while you walk to the exam. Exams and blue books are passed out, and the room monitor announces that you can begin.

Most exams are at least 3 to 4 hours of essay-type answers. A single exam question may be more than one typewritten page long. When the monitor eventually calls time and demands that everyone turn in their blue books, you realize that even with the 4 hours allotted, and after having set a land speed record for pen against paper, you ran out of time before completing your last answer. You go home, totally drained, for a few hours of rest and begin studying for the next exam. Repeat four times, and you will have made it through the first year of law school.

Final exams are exhausting in every way—mentally, emotionally, and physically. You put everything you have into them because they are the one chance you have to prove yourself. There are no other tests during the semester. Until grades come in, you have no way to judge how you are doing. Every student in the class is accustomed to academic success. If they were not, they would not have made it to law school. Past laurels are of little use, and relying on them is a mistake. However bitter a pill this is to swallow, by definition one out of every two students will be in the bottom half of the class for the first time.

Every effort is made to preserve privacy in grading. Grades may be posted by Social Security number or by randomly assigned test number. Our TQ wisely warned us not to do postmortems after exams and to talk about grades as little as possible. Comparing can cause hurt feelings, possibly your own. In the microcosm of law school, class standing can seem like everything to the vision of law school success. When you face this prospect, it is wise to remember that law school achievements do not dictate the success of a law practice and have little, if anything, to do with personal worth. Maintaining a healthy sense of proportion is essential.

Nevertheless, the hard fact is that grades do affect recruiting. Most law schools have placement offices that bring students together with potential employers. If grade point average is not the first thing an employer looks at, it is probably the second. Employer competition has caused major law firms to pursue the most promising students during their first year of school with increasing frequency. These students will be interviewed during the spring of their first year and offered summer jobs based on their backgrounds and first-semester or midterm grades. For most students, recruiting is a topic still reserved until the second year. Those students who do not have full-time jobs should consider attending summer school. Summer school is a chance to bring those grades up before the all-important start of the second year.

Second Year
(You want me to make decisions about the rest of my life *now?*)

The second year of law school reintroduces you to the concept of choices. There will be more decisions to make than you will know what to do with. You are on your own. In the second year, you begin to pick your own curriculum, allowing yourself to study areas that interest you or spark a specialization. You can select subjects that vary from advanced constitutional law and federal courts to environmental law and land-use planning to the taxation of oil and gas and bankruptcy law. A normal schedule includes about five courses that each meet for an hour, three times a week, and last for only one semester. Classes will contain a mix of second- and third-year students, with no differentiation. In making your course selections, seek guidance from other students about the courses and the professors. Also seek guidance from practicing attorneys about what areas of law have a promising future, both short-term and long-term.

Classroom instruction may seem geared more toward giving a substantive understanding of the subject matter, but your study schedule might be as vigorous as it was during the first year. You still must worry about outlining and about final exams that will be just as long and just as exhausting as they were at the end of the first year. You still must worry about grades. Ninety percent of the class will be trying to bring their grades up, and the other 10 percent will be trying to keep their grades up. However, during the busy second year of law school, students manage their academic efforts while they also begin other law school activities, take part-time clerking jobs in the community, and begin to interview for full-time summer jobs. Remember, you don't have to do everything at once.

One of the activities available is working with student publications. Many law schools have one or more student publications called law journals, some of which have national reputations. Membership on a law journal staff may be earned through making very high first-year grades or by participating in a writing competition. Students who accept an invitation to join a law journal staff will have to fulfill certain writing requirements. Generally, they will have to write one or more publishable legal articles. Student articles of exceptional quality will be published in the journal along with articles solicited from practicing attorneys and judges. Third-year journal members may serve on the editorial board, handling duties related to the content of the journal or editing papers and working with nonstaff authors.

Participation on a law journal can be time-consuming, and some students will pass up the opportunity even after being invited to join. Many attorneys who look back on journal work feel that it improved their research and writing skills, gave them experience in supervising the work of others, and impressed potential employers. The decision about whether or not to join should be made with the following considerations in mind: the reputation of the law journal, the amount of time membership requires, the comradery of the journal staff, the extent of your prior writing experience, and your desire to pursue other activities.

© 1984 by Sam Hurt

Mock trial and moot court competitions offer students the opportunity for advocacy experience. As the name implies, mock trial simulates a courtroom trial, with student teams representing either the "plaintiff" or the "defendant." Other students play the roles of witnesses. Cases are presented before a judge who presides over the trial and rules on evidentiary objections. The judge is usually a practicing attorney who, at the conclusion of the trial, will critique both teams and declare a winner. Moot court is much the same, but it simulates argument before an appellate judge who reviews the decision of a lower court and listens to presentations of opposing counsel on both the facts and the law.

For the winning team, participation in an oral advocacy competition can be very time-consuming. When a mock trial or moot court team wins, it advances to the next round of competition. In addition to preparation and practice time, a successful team may compete three or four nights each week for a month. As a team advances in the competition, it may have the opportunity to present its case before real judges. Teams at the top of their school's competition compete with one another for state titles, and state winners may compete for national honors. It is not uncommon for local practitioners or competition-sponsoring law firms to donate cash or other awards for the winners. Points accumulated along the way also may earn students membership in organizations such as the Order of the Barristers, a national organization of student legal advocates.

Again, if you are willing to devote the time required, the experience gained can be invaluable. Many top student competitors get their start during the second year of school, but novice competitions are available to students who want to participate but prefer to wait until their third year. A friend of mine who won her school's mock trial competition commented that the personal feedback from the judges who critiqued her was immensely more valuable than any lecture on, or even demonstration of, advocacy skills.

Recruiting season, in a fashion reminiscent of undergraduate fall rush, is one of the biggest events of the second year. Students begin their second year of law school armed with immaculate resumes and new interview wardrobes ready to meet the many firms who will visit their campus to recruit next year's summer law clerks. Summer law clerks, also known as summer associates, will work for these law firms full-time during the summer break before their third year. Many students who take summer positions with law firms split their summers by working six weeks at one firm and six weeks at another, often in different cities. Government agencies and corporations also send recruiting teams to law school campuses.

Participation in on-campus recruiting can be a lot of fun, but a thick suit of emotional armor is a good complement to the resume and wardrobe. Although some students manage to remain somewhat detached from all of the hullabaloo, many are absorbed by it, running the danger of forgetting that they are students first and interviewees second. The rational approach to interviewing is to target employers for whom you would ultimately be comfortable working. As with many human endeavors, however, prestige and status may play a major role. Success is measured, in part, by how many offers you have and with whom. It is not uncommon for a student to schedule three or four interviews a week for five or six straight weeks. Simple multiplication makes the potential for rejection obvious.

A model recruiting adventure goes something like this. A day and time are prearranged for you to interview between classes at the law school's placement office with two representatives of a major law firm. Whether or not a law firm is "major" in this sense depends on name recognition, number of attorneys, and salaries offered both to summer associates and to permanent hires. The interview lasts 20 to 30 minutes. You may also be invited to a lavish cocktail and dinner party that the firm is hosting that evening for its most promising candidates.

Very shortly, you might receive an invitation to visit the law firm's office at the firm's expense. You fly into town the night before, and reservations are held for you at one of the best hotels. Several of the attorneys take you for dinner and drinks. The next day you go to the firm's office and interview with several more attorneys. Lunch will be at one of the private clubs that the firm's attorneys frequent. You have more interviews in the afternoon and then fly home. An offer of employment as a summer associate follows shortly at a salary of $750 to $1,000 a week, depending on regional differences in the "market."

Six or more of these trips in a semester are not uncommon. Unfortunately, the opportunities to enjoy such model adventures are open primarily to those with first-year grades in the the top 20 percent of their class. The rest of the class is interviewing with smaller firms or for positions in alternate practices, or they are not interviewing through the school's placement office at all. Out-of-town office visits may be rare or nonexistent and salaries may be considerably lower. A new recruiting season starts in the spring for students who have not found the jobs they want and have the energy to keep looking for firms that have not filled all their positions.

In most instances, as fall finals approach, offers must be accepted or rejected. The vast majority of students who work as summer associates will later accept a permanent offer with the firm they worked for during the summer. Likewise, many firms rely on their summer associate programs to fill their upcoming permanent positions. Deciding how to spend the summer clearly can be momentous. With one year of law school under your belt, you are expected to consider factors like the kind of law you want to practice, the firm's ability to offer advancement in that area during the next two years, salary and bonus plans, the firm's physical facilities, the firm's method of associate supervision and training, billable hour requirements, how many associates earn a partnership position and how soon, and, perhaps most important, whether you will be happy working with the people at the firm. Picking the city in which you want to live will be the easy part. The opportunities will be exciting.

When spring arrives, many students take part-time clerking jobs at law firms in the town where their school is located. Law clerks generally work 15 to 20 hours a week after and between classes. They do legal research, draft motions and pleadings, and research documents, among other things. Like all attorneys, their time is recorded and billed to the client. Spring clerking jobs have several benefits. Many firms use their part-time clerkships as part of their recruitment programs. When summer jobs are not available, accepting a spring clerking position can get your foot in the door at a firm you are interested in working for after graduation. What you learn from a clerking position can give you a head start on adjusting to a summer job. You get paid. More important, however, a clerking position can be your first glimpse at what the practice of law is really like. The saying goes, if you like law school too much, you won't enjoy practicing. For many students who have not been overly impressed with law school, clerking is a refreshing reminder of why they are there.

Summer associates do the same type of work that clerks do during the school year, but the experience can be a very different one. Firms who hire summer associates generally emphasize recruiting their summer employees for permanent positions. More attention is paid to bringing summer associates along to hearings, depositions, appellate arguments, and client meetings. A lot more attention is paid to entertainment.

Summer associates evaluate their firms on such items as client contact, number of hours worked in an average week, quality of feedback, and the important category of firm social events. My favorite summer events were a wine-tasting party at a senior lawyer's home, a trip to hear Lou Rawls under the stars in Dallas, Texas, and various boating excursions. A friend of mine recalls fondly the time one firm took him to a popular lake resort for the weekend.

© 1984 by Sam Hurt

The summer recruiting game is grabbing the top salaries, going to parties, and doing as little real work as possible. Not all students work for firms that play the game. Many smaller firms cannot afford it. But most firms who hire summer associates do try to keep their salaries competitive with other firms their size and encourage social interaction with the attorneys.

Enjoy, but remember that if recruiting can be likened to fraternity or sorority rush, an associateship after graduation can be compared to a seven-year pledgeship. Doing high-quality work and showing responsibility will give you staying power. The goal of summer associates is to have an offer of permanent employment with a firm they like before the third year of law school begins.

Third Year
(What do you mean, graduating isn't enough?)

Graduation will be in sight as the third year begins. Third year really is not boring, but the challenges have become more familiar. You still have law journal and advocacy activities to pursue, you still can improve your grade average, and you still must suffer through exams. When you make course selections, you may want to take subjects that will be covered on the bar exam. This can vary from state to state. For example, the Texas bar exam covers oil and gas law but not tax law, as does the Pennsylvania bar exam. It helps to save the toughest bar exam subjects for the last semester so that they will be fresh in your mind, but be sure that you will be able to secure a place in class when the time comes. There were so many panicked third-year students demanding enrollment in the law of wills and estates during my last semester that the school set up a video camera in the lecture hall so that some of us could watch by closed-circuit television in an adjacent room. It was inconvenient, but for once we had no worries about being called on in class.

Many third-year students will have accepted permanent offers before the end of the fall semester. Many others will still be interviewing. Which group you belong to has a lot to do with how much you relax and enjoy your last year. For those still looking for a permanent position, taking part-time clerking jobs can be very important. Having an income, of course, is helpful to almost every student. However, those who have secured their after-graduation job and who may have a sizable signing bonus in the bank may prefer to relax at a beach or in the mountains instead of work. In a way, the third year of law school seems like a final taste of freedom before dedication to a new career.

Finishing your last law school exam will bring an indescribable feeling of relief, of closure, and of self-satisfaction. Storing away outlines, shelving used texts, and throwing away old class notes have definite sacred and ceremonial overtones. Your graduation exercises will really mean something to you this time. In an age when an undergraduate degree has become almost expected, a law degree is still a very special accomplishment, and you will know in your heart that you really earned the pride of family and friends. At least one thing about law school graduation will be like all other graduations, however. It will bring the familiar sad farewells to friends and classmates. After all, you may not see them again until next month when bar exam prep classes begin.

When you do see your old law school chums at those classes, more than likely you will retire with them to philosophical discussions around the cold beverage of choice, and someone will pose the ultimate Socratic inquiry, "After everything that we've been through during the past three years, shouldn't just graduating from law school be enough?"

THE TUNNEL AT THE END OF THE LIGHT
Taking the Bar Exam

William D. Barwick

William D. Barwick takes a different look at the bar exam, the final, frightening monster in the law school horror flick. His perspective offers a fresh, upbeat approach to surviving the multistate and essay portions of the exam. From the history of the bar to practical tips on taking the test ("have a candy bar handy"), Barwick brings to this dreaded ordeal new insight and a good sense of humor.

You've seen the plot device used dozens of times in recent horror movies—*Aliens, Poltergeist, Friday the 13th, Ishtar.* The hero or heroine reaches some haven of safety after repeated death-defying trials and escapes, and the villain/monster has apparently been disintegrated once and for all. Our protagonists breathe a sigh of relief and hug each other, and even the music tends to lull the audience into a feeling of safety. But wait! Beneath the bed, in the closet, or behind the door, the "THING" (or what's left of it) waits for one last leap, slobbering and snarling its way across the screen for a final life-or-death assault on our stars.

Welcome to the bar exam. After three mind-numbing years of frustration, terror, and alternating boredom and panic, just when you thought it was safe to go back in the water, here comes the test that can tell you in an instant whether or not the monster has truly been disintegrated once and for all. This chapter attempts to examine the history of this ordeal, its psychological impact, its overall function in the process of legal education, and its possible violation of the Constitution's Eighth Amendment prohibiting cruel and unusual punishment.

William D. Barwick is with Sutherland, Asbill & Brennan in Atlanta, Georgia. He has written numerous articles for local, state, and national periodicals and intends to start working for a living soon.

27

History of the Bar Exam

Bar examinations are the vestigial remains of trial by torture. Just as one could disprove a charge of sorcery by holding one's breath for several minutes underwater, one could prove oneself worthy of professional status by writing Latin prose for two straight days without developing writer's cramp. In later feudal times, an ecclesiastical question was added to the exam, requiring candidates to determine how many angels could dance on the head of a pin without being considered an unlawful assembly. Ultimately, those wishing to become litigators were also required to endure an additional trial by combat, but this usually only required the perfunctory bludgeoning of a serf.

The bar exam continued in this form for almost 700 years. In the same century that brought us the development of the machine gun, nerve gas, C-Span, and nuclear weapons, however, a new wrinkle was added to the time-honored ordeal: the multistate multiple choice exam, a new suspense angle in that great horror film, "Will I—Did I—Dare I Find Out If I Passed the Bar Exam?" This will be discussed in more detail below.

The Horror, the Horror

Why do law students so dread the bar exam? For that matter, why don't turkeys celebrate Thanksgiving? Actually, it can be taken repeatedly in most states, so failure isn't usually career ending. Many large law firms will actually pay you hundreds of dollars a week just to sit in the library and study law, a privilege that many law students mowed lawns for three years to enjoy. What's the big deal?

Well, first of all, if you don't pass, your grade will not just appear anonymously next to a Social Security number on a bulletin board. The winners get their names published in the local paper, and the rolls are usually pored over by contemporaries as though they were the survivor lists from a major shipwreck. Second, throughout your entire legal career an invisible asterisk will always appear next to your name—on pleadings, firm stationery, even Martindale-Hubbell, the national directory of law firms. No matter what level of greatness you achieve, like Roger Maris there will always be that tainted footnote: "Failed bar exam on first try."

Finally, there is the wait before you know the results. In modern human experience, the only thing that takes longer than grading a bar exam is the professional basketball season. This extended period also allows for the proliferation of rumors: "The examiners lost all the booklets from the second day and they're throwing the whole test out"; "I've heard that only 38 percent will pass"; or "A lawsuit is being filed by Alabama graduates because of cultural bias." These and more will take on a life of their own, so beware.

How to Take the Bar Exam—
Do I Ask For a Blindfold or Not?

By the time most law students complete formal education, they will have taken approximately 2,000 standardized multiple choice tests. Do not think for a moment that this will prepare you for the multistate portion of the exam, in which your chances will be statistically worse than in Russian roulette.

You can try all the things your high school and college teachers taught you about taking the SAT and LSAT: get a good night's sleep, bring twenty-three sharpened No. 2 pencils, have a candy bar handy, etc. Some law school graduates employ additional techniques. Some will wear suits and carry briefcases (containing candy bars). Look professional, feel professional, be professional! Or you can wear a loincloth, pump yourself full of Mexican food, and listen to the Grateful Dead on your Walkman. It really won't make that much difference.

A typical multistate question looks like this:

A witness testifies that she believes the light was red at the intersection because the police officer told her it was. An objection to this answer should be sustained:

(a)   because the testimony is hearsay;
(b)   because the testimony is hearsay;
(c)   because the testimony is hearsay;
(d)   because the testimony is hearsay.

Looks like fun, doesn't it? Actually the correct answer is (d), because it has a period at the end instead of a semicolon. For the sum of $300, a bar review course will teach you this and several other tricks that will increase your chances from none to slim.

After you have finished the multistate, there will be a false sense of relief. You know that the next one or two days of the exam will be essay questions only, and any good law student knows that if you are totally ignorant about a particular topic, an essay question is your best chance. Like an infinite number of monkeys at an infinite number of typewriters, most law students feel that a completed blue book will probably (and accidentally) contain a sufficient number of buzzwords that are tangentially related to the issues in question.

Do not let this sense of relief deceive you, however, for there is one big difference between law school essay exams and the essay portion of the bar exam. When you walk into a classroom prepared to take your criminal procedure final, you can usually rely upon the questions dealing solely with crime and punishment. You do not spend the first 15 minutes on each question deciding whether it also includes a Uniform Commercial Code sales issue or whether you should discuss the rule against perpetuities. Veteran bar examiners invariably have war stories about would-be lawyers who, for example, write brilliant dissertations on riparian water rights in response to questions about a slip-and-fall accident in a supermarket.

The essay portion of the exam has one redeeming value—it resembles real life. In law school, it would be considered unfair to ask you to answer questions on an exam dealing with divorce law when you have not taken a domestic relations course. Once you are a lawyer, both clients and friends will have no reluctance in asking you detailed questions about a past, pending, or prospective divorce, and they will be disappointed when you respond that you are a tax lawyer and never took that course in law school. Of the above two situations, the bar exam is more like the actual practice of law, and if the bar exam becomes disappointed in your response, it can ruin more than your whole day.

The techniques of taking the exam aren't nearly as important as preparation, but be sure to follow these important rules: (1) go armed in case the person next to you smokes or chews gum; (2) have a name that starts with "A" or "B" so you can sit in the front of the room and not see the mass of humanity trying to deprive you of a livelihood; and (3) never, never, never discuss the completed questions and answers during bathroom breaks or at the end of the exam.

© 1982 by Sam Hurt

Preparation—Don't Panic, Just Remember That You Will Be Responsible for Seven Centuries of Accumulated Jurisprudence

Preparation is far more important than technique, but it is inevitable that you will know a couple of people who tell you that they're taking the exam "cold." If these people truly do such a thing and pass the exam, your only hope is that they die young from a lingering and painful disease. Most students who brag that they are going to take the exam without studying are lying, however, and it is likely that they will eventually leave the practice to become investment bankers or presidential advisers.

Your bar review course should be state oriented, since passing the multistate is only slightly less probable than being born a Rockefeller. Different states have one- or two-day essay sessions, and it is inevitable that one or more questions will involve legal matters peculiar to a particular state. In Georgia, for instance, one essay question several years ago asked the following: "You have just successfully defended a client on a moonshine-trafficking charge, and your fee is $5,000. How many Ball jars should the fee fill?" Obviously, Cornell Law graduates who took a national bar review course had some difficulty with this question. Make your decision accordingly.

Before you even select a bar review course, however, an even weightier decision must be made. Many states allow law students to take the bar exam during their third year. Because of the intense pressure of preparation, however, you must ask yourself several questions before you opt to take the early bar exam. First, have you used up all of the elective courses that are your law school's "guts"? You may regret having taken "The Philosophy of Justice" from old Dr. Webfoot during spring semester of your second year, but at the time it was important to start dating members of the opposite sex again.

Second, if you've passed the bar by the time you graduate, will the sweatshop that bought your soul for $60,000 a year want an immediate return on its investment? The period of time between law school graduation and the beginning of work will be your last opportunity to get rid of that pasty look you acquired during your first year.

Finally, what is the attitude of the teachers at your law school toward the early bar exam? Many law professors feel that the early exam is an infringement upon their academic time with third-year students and resent it bitterly. This is somewhat unrealistic, since their academic time with third-year students is daily infringed upon by "Magnum" reruns and "Wheel of Fortune." Other law professors are more tolerant, particularly the ones who hold the local bar exam study review franchises. All law school professors, however, are profoundly envious of any exam that does not have to be graded for at least four months.

Is This Really Necessary, Or Could I Just Beat Myself over the Head with a Bat Instead?

Believe it or not, bar exams may not be necessary. They aren't used, for example, in Wisconsin if you are a graduate of an ABA-accredited law school. Has anybody lately noticed an outbreak of murder and pillage among Wisconsin lawyers? Is America less safe because there are no essay questions on the Wisconsin bar exam regarding brewery or cheese law?

Each state still jealously guards its control over the practice of law. Of course, most states also jealously guard the licensing of beauticians and undertakers, so we shouldn't feel too put upon by the rigors of the bar exam. As long as the requirement remains, however, three things should be kept in mind as you prepare for this final ordeal in your journey to professional practice. First, you *will* pass the exam. This is not true for some of you, but you won't be the ones reading this book. Second, exactly one minute after learning that you've passed the bar exam, you will have completely forgotten the agony involved. In fact, this author was forced to undergo deep hypnosis to recall most of the factual background contained in this chapter.

Finally, the format you choose for celebrating the successful completion of the exam is insignificant. It will be your life's best: (a) drunk; (b) dinner; (c) sex; (d) sleep for three days; or (e) thanksgiving worship service at your church, synagogue, or mosque. In any event, you won't need a bar review course to guess the correct answer to the previous multiple choice quiz.

In closing, the author wishes to note that the hyperbole in this chapter should not unnecessarily deter you from a legal career, for the bar exam is really quite bearable and certainly not insurmountable. Indeed, at some point in your legal career, as you open your local bar journal to gaze upon the 500 or so names of hungry young lawyers recently admitted to practice in your state, you will say to yourself, "Why the heck don't they get tough on that blasted bar exam?"

POSTPONING REALITY
Judicial Clerkships

Justice Alva Hugh Maddox

Justice Alva Hugh Maddox of the Alabama Supreme Court takes a practical and realistic look at one alternative to jumping directly into the legal arena after law school. He offers practical advice about obtaining and enjoying a clerkship position and insight on how judges use and perceive their clerks. The Justice emphasizes the lifelong friendships developed and closes with summations of former law clerks' impressions of their clerking experience.

There is no guarantee that a lawyer who begins a legal career as a judicial clerk will wind up on the state's highest court, but I highly recommend a clerkship. It gives the graduating young lawyer an opportunity to work at the elbow of a judge and to discuss principles of law and philosophies of government in actual controversies between people and people, or between people and their government, that the beginning lawyer may not deal with in a law practice for years.

A judicial clerkship is much like an internship; it offers law graduates an opportunity to work with actual cases and apply their academic knowledge to help the judge decide those cases. It is an opportunity to work in the real world of the law, with real controversies, on varied topics involving parties with conflicting interests.

The purpose of this chapter is to articulate in some detail what a judicial clerkship is like, what the role of judicial clerks is in the judicial system, and what judges usually expect of their clerks. I have drawn heavily on my own experience as a judicial clerk to two judges, and because I am now a judge I have tried to state what I think most judges expect of their judicial clerks. I have set out why I think that a judicial clerkship can

Justice Alva Hugh Maddox is an associate justice of the Supreme Court of Alabama. He served as a judicial clerk to the late Judge Aubrey M. Cates of the Alabama Court of Appeals and then to United States District Court Judge Frank M. Johnson Jr.

be valuable experience to a young lawyer, not only in the administration of justice, but to the individual judicial clerk as well.

How a Judge Selects a Judicial Clerk

First, how does a judge select a judicial clerk? The selection process varies. Most judges prefer, of course, to find judicial clerks who have graduated at or near the top of their class, are academically inclined, like to do legal research, have the ability to write, and can commit at least a year to the job. Other considerations may also enter into the selection process, some totally unrelated to the law. The relationship between a judge and a law clerk becomes a very personal one. The two work together daily; enjoying each other's company is critical to a good working relationship.

Competition for Judicial Clerkships

How important are grades and class standing to a judge who is hiring a clerk? It varies. Some judges place great emphasis on grades, and grades are important, but they are not the most important factor for all judges. I always make a final decision after a personal interview, and, on balance, I prefer applicants who are well-rounded and have the ability to get along with other people. In my own case, Judge Aubrey Cates, even though a Rhodes scholar himself, did not make grades his sole criterion, or I might never have been hired.

Many judges, especially at the federal appellate level, give preference to graduates of the more prestigious law schools. All other things being equal, in Alabama judges usually prefer graduates of the state's two accredited law schools—the University of Alabama School of Law and Samford University's Cumberland School of Law—because, generally, graduates of those schools are more familiar with Alabama law and practice. Some judges prefer to have judicial clerks with law review experience, but there is usually stiff competition with law firms for those in the top 10 percent of their class and with law review experience.

Most of the time, a judge will have many applicants for every vacancy. Federal judges can pay their judicial clerks more than state court judges, and, because law students often prefer to clerk in the federal system, the competition for available federal positions can be fierce. Similarly, there are more applicants for state judicial clerkships than there are jobs available. In both the federal and state systems, grades and research and writing experience are valuable assets.

Comparison of Trial and Appellate Clerkships

What does a judicial clerk do? It depends. First and foremost, it depends upon the desires and needs of the particular judge. It also depends on whether the judge is a trial or an appellate judge.

Judicial clerks to trial judges, while involved in a great deal of research, have many other duties, such as reviewing motions and making recommendations to the judge. They may review jury instructions requested by the parties and perform quick legal research for the judge as a trial progresses. While trial judges' clerks will not directly participate in a trial, they will listen to the evidence and learn tactics and strategy used by some of the best trial lawyers admitted to practice before the court. A judicial clerk in a trial court will be "in the pit," so to speak, and will see the parties, their attorneys, and the reactions of the witnesses and jurors to the matters being presented.

In the appellate court, there is little of the drama that can develop during a trial. Appellate clerks see the trial through a printed record and primarily research the law of a case. They have reading and writing jobs—living in the library and spending countless hours preparing memoranda of law for their judges. An appellate clerk deals with legal theory; a trial court judicial clerk functions in a trial atmosphere and performs a variety of functions. One works where the action is, the other works with the record of what occurred during the "action."

How Does a Judge Use a Clerk?

Some judges ask their clerks only to do legal research, others ask them to prepare memoranda summarizing the positions taken by the opposing parties (these are probably in the majority), and some use their clerks to prepare preliminary drafts of proposed opinions. Those judges who have their clerks prepare preliminary drafts are further subdivided into those who give the clerk little, if any, guidance beforehand and those who have periodic conferences on the case as the draft is being prepared. I follow the latter procedure most frequently, but when a clerk has demonstrated an ability to prepare a proposed opinion, I follow the former procedure. In either case, I sometimes make substantial changes in the draft. On other occasions, however, I may accept the draft substantially as written. It depends on the individual case, the quality of the draft, and the nature of the legal issue involved.

The Role and Influences of the Judicial Clerk

As judicial clerks have become increasingly important, disagreement has arisen as to what their role should be. One writer observed, "To some people, judicial clerks are part of a long and noble tradition. To a few others, they are 25-year-old Svengalis influencing the judicial process toward views inculcated into them by a phalanx of activist law professors." (D. Crump, "Law Clerks; Their Roles and Relations with Their Judges," *Judicature*, Vol. 69, No. 4, p. 236.)

In a comprehensive book on the role of judicial clerks, a former judicial clerk, John B. Oakley, writes, "In its ideal form, the judicial clerk is meant to fiddle with the law, to advocate innovation, to introduce to its inner sanctum the views of those outside." (J. Oakley and R. Thomson, *Law Clerks and the Judicial Process: Perceptions of the Qualities and Functions of Law Clerks in American Courts.*) Others disagree, contending that judicial clerks should not play such a vital role in the judicial process and that their role is one of research of what the law is, not of what the law ought to be (D. Crump, *Judicature*, as above, p. 237).

Judicial clerks can make excellent sounding boards for new ideas and many times offer the judge a new perspective. I tell my judicial clerks, especially those who have worked with me for a while and whose ability I trust, that I want them to disagree with me on legal points. I had one judicial clerk who, years after he left, said respectfully that he could never get me to agree with him on an evolving principle of law. That same clerk, however, did substantial research on an opinion that I consider one of my best.

As a former clerk, and now as a judge, I enjoy the intellectual exchange that occurs with my clerks when there is a hotly contested case. Sometimes I may ask them to play devil's advocate and point out the weaknesses in my legal argument. At the appellate level, of course, many cases are indeed hotly contested and may be decided by only one vote.

The Social Side of the Relationship

The close interpersonal relationship between clerk and judge often develops into a long-lasting friendship. Occasionally, a judge's former clerks will get together to honor the judge. As a former clerk to Judge Frank Johnson, I have attended three functions held for him. When I clerked for him, I was also invited to his annual Christmas party and his summer lake party. Former clerks of Pelham J. Merrill, who retired from our court in 1976, refer to themselves as the Merrill Gang, and they honor him from time to time, the latest being on his fiftieth wedding anniversary. My former clerks came back to Montgomery from as far away as Washington, D.C., and Miami, Florida, to honor me on the fifteenth year of my service on the court.

What the Judge Expects of the Clerk

Judicial clerks will work closely with their judge, and the judge must be able to place complete confidence in them. The judge has a right to expect that the clerk will be competent, honest, and loyal. Loyalty is paramount. Working at the judge's elbow, a judicial clerk learns a lot about the judge's habits, idiosyncrasies, likes and dislikes, and judicial philosophy. Many judges share very confidential views with their clerks, and these must never be divulged. Our clerks take an oath of confidentiality as a condition of employment.

"He used to be a nice guy . . . he didn't get to be so high and mighty 'til his appointment to the Federal bench."

Clerks' Impressions

In connection with this chapter, I asked each of my former staff attorneys and judicial clerks to state briefly their impressions about the job. Several responded, and Keith Norman, a former staff attorney who is now associate director of the Alabama State Bar, summed it up best when he said:

> "Perhaps at no other time in my legal career will I possess the opportunity to have as direct an impact upon the jurisprudence of Alabama as I did while clerking for the Alabama Supreme Court."

Others stated:

> "A judicial clerkship is a practical and beneficial way to bridge the gap between the academics of law school and the private practice of law."
>
> **—Edward M. Patterson, attorney,**
> **Montgomery, Alabama**

> "I came away from my year as a clerk with the realization that the law is not an abstract theory found in treaties or hornbooks, but that it touches the lives and fortunes of real people."
>
> **—George C. Garikes, attorney,**
> **Washington, D.C.**

> "My clerkship made the law come alive."
>
> **—Raymond P. Fitzpatrick Jr., attorney,**
> **Birmingham, Alabama**

> "Clerkship is the beginning of a friendship."
>
> **—George M. Grant, attorney,**
> **Washington, D.C.**

> "In my opinion, there is no better training for a young attorney, particularly one interested in the scholarly aspects of the law, than an appellate clerkship. Only in such a position can one be exposed to such a wide variety of legal issues in such a relatively short time. The opportunity to work closely with distinguished jurists gives the judicial clerk valuable insight into the process of judicial decision making as well as the intricacies of the appellate process."
>
> **—C. Jeffrey Ash, attorney,**
> **Montgomery, Alabama**

THE MANY FACES OF PRACTICE

READY, YOUR HONOR
Litigation Practice

Michael J. McManus

Courtroom gladiator and proud of it, Michael J. McManus gives you a glimpse of what litigation practice is all about. His account of the incredible ups and downs that go with the job is replete with the high level of humor that is the hallmark and the respite of many a good litigator.

So you want to be a litigator—suing the bad guys and defending all the innocent lambs. You will call yourself, and be called by others, everything from a stand-up trial lawyer to a stand-up comic, mouthpiece, warrior, hired gun, perpetrator of evil, and defender of the faith. In a few short months, you can go from representing beautiful and helpless orphan children injured by corrupt aircraft corporations to defending chemical companies against middle-class families claiming to be injured by terrible toxins. Contradictory? No. It's just litigation. And, unlike those who have engaged themselves in the also noble tasks of drafting incomprehensible merger statements and interpreting mindless tax provisions, you will have fun. If you don't, you are not truly a litigator, because there is no other sane reason to take on this kind of job.

You might ask what in the world makes litigators think they are so special. After all, aren't the litigators clogging up the court system, wasting valuable public resources? Aren't litigators driving up insurance rates and health-care costs right off the charts? Wouldn't litigators sell their very souls to the devil to win, simply for winning's sake? The answer to each of these questions is a resounding no.

Although, as with any profession or group, there are a few bad apples, the vast majority of litigators are responsible, ethical, and professional.

Michael J. McManus is a litigation partner in Jackson & Campbell, P.C., in Washington. A graduate of Notre Dame and Tulane, Mr. McManus's practice is now focused on toxic tort and product liability litigation. He has handled complex litigation for clients as diverse as the Virginia State Police and survivors of an airplane crash.

Good litigators enable their clients to have access to our court system for the orderly resolution of disputes; good litigators assist our judicial system in bringing about worthy social change on behalf of the common good; good litigators are essential to the smooth and fair functioning of our judicial system; and good litigators protect and preserve our civil liberties and civil rights. These are awesome tasks and responsibilities, perhaps likely to bring snickers and skeptical smiles from the ignorant and uninformed, but those who have kept one innocent person out of jail or recovered even $500 for someone who has been injured know that theirs is a most necessary, and therefore most rewarding, task.

To prospective lawyers, the term "rewarding" may light up the eyes. It should, but perhaps not for the monetary reasons you might be imagining. No doubt a number of litigators have practices that are exceptionally rewarding in dollars and cents. In every major metropolitan area in this country, there are usually one or two plaintiffs' lawyers, or firms, that somehow get all of the golden personal injury cases. It seems as though every week another million-dollar verdict is won, earning those plaintiffs' attorneys more cars, longer boats, and better antiques for the office. I would hazard a guess, however, that most of the litigators I know still would wade into the arena of the courtroom without those types of significant monetary rewards, and, in fact, most do. It's the nature of the beast.

Litigation, whether involving a $5,000 fender bender or a $50,000 insurance dispute, can be an awful lot of fun, but rarely, if ever, is it easy. It shouldn't be. Litigators carry with them an awesome responsibility that, at times, can be overwhelming. Absent flagrant violations of certain rules, it is clients and not attorneys who go to jail or lose their business or their life's savings. Litigators have an ethical obligation to subordinate any and all personal considerations to the goal of protecting and furthering their clients' valid interests.

The Right Stuff

What does it take to be a litigator, and how and where do you start? Most litigators were not born a Perry Mason or a Ben Matlock. If not blessed with the necessary talents, you must develop them—intuition, imagination, integrity, a sense of humor, perseverance, organization, flexibility, dedication to the client, confidence, a skin as tough as elephant hide, a poker face that Robin Williams couldn't crack, and even a little bit of acting ability. Add to that some basic legal research and writing skills and a working knowledge of the rules of evidence and procedure, and you will have a modest beginning. Next comes hard work.

The best ways to fulfill your duties and responsibilities to your clients are to be prepared, be prepared, and be prepared; and to be truly prepared can be a grueling task. Before the first words of any brilliant oratory are uttered, and before the first teardrop falls in response to a moving closing argument, a great deal of groundwork must be laid. Depending on the complexities of the case, for every hour spent in the thrill of courtroom battle there may be hundreds, sometimes thousands, of hours spent on tedious, difficult, and even boring tasks. The prepared lawyer must study every document, every word of every deposition, all relevant legal authority, and each argument advanced by opposing counsel. Case law must be analyzed and dissected. Facts must be evaluated from every conceivable angle. While crafting an imaginative position based on all of this information is indeed challenging and exciting, much of the underlying work is not. In fact, oftentimes it is downright torturous, but it must be done.

Anyone who has had medicine prescribed knows that the first qualification for being a doctor is to have failed penmanship. Just try reading hundreds of pages of doctor's "notes" in a serious medical malpractice case, a task comparable to capital punishment and usually meted out to first- and second-year associates in law firms. Follow that up by reading a plaintiff's deposition in a case involving a complex tort matter, where the most stimulating questions involve the type of carpeting in the plaintiff's house, or an excruciatingly detailed accounting of each and every time he had bloodshot eyes, spotty lungs, and excess gas. If you still haven't had enough fun, you always can review the insurance policies involved in a multimillion-dollar coverage dispute. After spending hours diagraming each and every sentence of those documents, drafted, it seems, by the same people who are now driving taxicabs in major cities, you can reach but one conclusion, or two, or possibly three. The insured has either paid $2-million for no coverage at all or now is the proud owner of one half of the first party of the second part, depending on the deductible by reference therein, or both of the above, maybe.

War Stories

Tedious as it may seem, this kind of work is essential, and often it leads to the golden nuggets of information that bring the greatest reward. I once represented a woman who had been assaulted grievously by a young punk released from a state juvenile detention facility. It was our position that the facility's personnel had been grossly negligent in prematurely releasing this modern-day Jack the Ripper, who had cut our client's throat and left her to die. Miraculously she survived, and we pursued an action against the state employees who were responsible for letting "Jack" go.

43

Every obstacle was thrown in our path, and although we felt we had a compelling case, we still searched for a "smoking gun." Finally, after several depositions, numerous interrogatories, and a multitude of interviews and telephone calls, we discovered that certain documents that we had been led to believe did not exist were stored less than a mile from the courthouse. In the middle of one night, while the trial was progressing, telephone calls to various officials were made and arrangements accomplished to get the original documents delivered to the courthouse. Over rigorous objection by the defendant's counsel, the court admitted into evidence the original school records of the perpetrator of the crime. Contrary to the picture of innocence and unfortunate social circumstance painted by the state's representative, these school records revealed a dangerous felon who, from the first grade on, had physically and brutally attacked fellow students and teachers and finally was expelled permanently in the ninth grade for inciting a riot. The drudgery and tediousness of the search for this smoking gun was critical to the jury returning a substantial verdict and award to our client.

All litigators will have their stories about cases won that never should have been and cases lost that couldn't possibly have been. It is a fact of life to a litigator that, while the vast majority of cases are settled by compromise, for those that go to trial there is but one winner and one loser, and even the best lawyers lose on occasion. Sometimes, even hard work and all of your best efforts are not enough.

Not every story ends up a happy one, and, indeed, our Jack the Ripper case eventually did not. As we knew would happen, the state appealed the jury verdict to the Supreme Court of Virginia. All of the depositions, all of the pleadings, and the hundreds of pages of documents had to be reviewed and learned again, and now hundreds of pages of the trial transcript as well. Hours of legal research and hours of frantic drafting of briefs to meet tight deadlines and printing schedules were followed by months of waiting. Then came time for oral arguments to the Supreme Court—for which everything had to be reread and relearned—followed by more months of waiting for the court's decision.

Through all of this ordeal, we were confident that our hard-fought jury verdict would be preserved. After all, the verdict was reached on jury instructions proposed by the state and approved by the trial judge. The verdict clearly was supported by all of the evidence and testimony, was affirmed by a thoughtful and well-written decision of the trial court denying defendant's motions for a new trial, and was totally consistent with then, and I emphasize "then," existing law. Unfortunately the then-existing law was not enough. The Supreme Court reversed the jury verdict by expanding a doctrine of law to give immunity from liability for the acts of social workers and detention facility personnel hired by the state. Although we eventually were able to secure repayment to the client for her medical and out-of-pocket expenses by way of a special bill passed by the state legislature, hundreds and hundreds of hours had been spent on the case, reflected only by an empty and disappointed feeling.

© 1982 by Michael Goodman

An important aspect of life as a litigator is dealing with the incredible highs and enormously depressing lows, joined together by innumerable challenges, rewards, tensions, and frustrations, all of which go with the job. Some brief examples follow.

You have just spent two weeks in trial, and the jury has been deliberating for four days. You can hear the jury members shouting at each other through the doors, but they are hopelessly deadlocked. The judge is ready to declare a mistrial, but you take the big gamble. The jury has reported it is deadlocked, six to one, but the judge does not ask which way it is leaning. With your client's consent, you propose to defendant's counsel that you will both abide by the decision of six, and not the usual seven, jurors. To your utter shock and amazement defense counsel agrees, and you now know that he is just as convinced of having six jurors on his side as you are.

The jurors are called into the courtroom and told that if they still are deadlocked six to one, then they are to retire to the jury room and return a verdict in favor of the party with six votes. They are told further that if the verdict on defendant's liability is for the plaintiff, your client, those six are to determine the amount of compensation to be awarded him, an often time-consuming task. The jurors file back into the jury room, and you literally hold your breath, knowing that if they return before you turn blue you have lost the case. The seconds, seeming like hours, pass by; you can no longer hold your breath. The jury has not returned, and you know that you and your client have won.

Or consider a case in which your client, a defendant in an automobile accident case, has rear-ended the plaintiff, who happened to be six months pregnant at the time of the accident. Your client is a salt-of-the-earth woman, as honest as the day is long, but, unfortunately for both of you, just as negligent. You have offered the plaintiff thousands of dollars to settle, but it appears that she is looking to make this case her retirement fund. Thankfully, her child was born healthy and uninjured. It becomes apparent during the trial, however, that while the plaintiff made a big deal about her mental anguish and distress over her unborn child, she never went to visit her pediatrician or her OB/GYN after the accident. The plaintiff was clearly reaching for too much, and you point this out to the jury. The jury finds in favor of the plaintiff, as it must pursuant to the judge's instructions, but the jurors have seen your point. You are elated, particularly since this is your first trial, as you hear the foreman read the words ". . . and we award damages in the amount of one dollar."

Finally, you have just spent two weeks in North Dakota trying a case where the outside temperature is a brisk −40°. It is a product liability case involving allegations of toxic chemical exposure, and on the night before closing argument the tragedy in Bhopal, India, occurs. Representing a chemical company in New York, you have just argued to the jury that you had such faith in your client's product and the North Dakota judicial system that you chose to present your defense to the jury, rather than settle the case as your codefendants had done. While the jury is deliberating its verdict, your client's insurance carrier calls from New York City and literally orders you to settle the case, at whatever price it takes. The incredulous plaintiffs happily accept your generous offer, and the trial judge, just as happily, threatens to fine you thousands of dollars for wasting the court's and the jury's time on a case that, if it were going to be settled, should have been dispensed with before the trial began.

The jury's deliberation is interrupted, and it is advised of the settlement. A few minutes later you are politely asked to join the jurors in their room, and a broad grin crosses the judge's face as he pushes you in the door. Your only hope is that they heed your pleas for mercy before they tar and feather you and run you out of town. Fortunately, they give you an opportunity to explain what has just occurred, and since they have given two weeks of their life to this case you tell them everything; you tell them that the insurance carrier called the shots in this case and that because of the Indian disaster it was terrified that the North Dakota jury would return a runaway verdict against the chemical company.

You apologize, explain to them that you had confidence that they would decide the case fairly, and tell them that you have argued strenuously against any settlement. In fact, you were genuinely confident that they would have returned a verdict in your client's favor, and indeed they had. Moments before the bailiff entered their room to advise them of the settlement, they had completed their vote—12 to 0 in favor of your client. Some of the jurors were so impressed that they asked for the name of the nearest local distributor of your client's product. Although that verdict will never be recorded on the books, the civility and responsibility of that jury will never be forgotten. It all was worth it.

The Pace

The pace can be hectic, even frantic. In the span of one day you finally can receive that box of documents from your own client that, despite several assurances in response to all of your careful and precise questions about its business dealings, demonstrate that things aren't quite as the client represented—in fact, you wonder if you are even dealing with the same company! Then, after calling all the lawyers who haven't answered your interrogatories on time, and putting all the phone messages from those lawyers to whom you owe answers to interrogatories at the bottom of the pile, you madly dash off to the courthouse for your status conference with the judge who last month fined five lawyers $100 apiece for being 2 minutes late to his courtroom. The cab is stuck in traffic, so you run the last two blocks to the courthouse, arriving drenched in perspiration and on the verge of cardiac arrest and/or a stroke, just at the appointed minute. Forty minutes later, the judge casually strolls onto the bench murmuring something about other court business in chambers and then proceeds to give you a trial date that coincides with the first day of your first vacation in three years.

Of course, the court's schedule is not run for the convenience of lawyers, and even though it matters to no one whether or not the case is tried three weeks earlier or three weeks later, it will go on as the judge has scheduled it. You then return to the office to find a letter from a client who says he would be happy to pay your now-six-month-overdue $40,000 bill incurred in saving him $5-million in liability, but politely inquiring why it took you 6 hours to prepare a key witness for his trial testimony. Couldn't you have done it in 5 1/2? Right under the message is the 150-page motion for summary judgment filed by opposing counsel in a case in Mississippi, whose quirky rules require a response in ten days. The sneaky devils who filed this abomination have mailed it "pony expired," so you really only have three days within which to research and draft your response. Your date with the by now very skeptical blonde is canceled for the third time in two weeks, and you bask in the glow of knowing that in four days, if nothing else happens, you will get some sleep. Heat up the coffeepot, and send in more Twinkies.

© 1985 by Michael Goodman

Sometimes the pace is not so fast, and day to day it can be about as stimulating as watching Della, Paul, and Perry on the 11 o'clock reruns. I once represented several orphans who had been injured severely in an airplane crash en route to their new adoptive homes. The defendant was a large American aircraft corporation that had all the money and all the time in the world. Every step of the litigation was met with motions, motions, and more motions. The defendants took depositions that on some occasions literally lasted for weeks. At one point, a witness lost her voice after several weeks of testifying from 9 a.m. to 6 p.m.

The children were examined by batteries of doctors for both sides, all of whom had to be deposed. Teachers, neighbors, relatives, and friends were deposed, in Washington, D.C., and in locations as exotic and far away as Bangkok, Thailand. Tens of thousands of pages of documents were produced, reproduced, and produced again. In the final months before the multiple trials began, 14- to 16-hour days, for seven days of the week, were the rule, not the exception. The trials took from three to five weeks to complete, and many were scheduled to begin within days of the completion of the prior one.

Following initial verdicts in favor of the children, more forests had to be cut to replenish the paper supply, more motions were filed, and then the inevitable appeals came rolling in. All of the verdicts were tossed out on evidentiary grounds, and new trials were ordered. There were then more depositions, more examinations, and more motions filed before the trials again commenced. After more trials, and still more motions, the cases finally were settled, over seven years after they had been filed. The children had gotten older, but the lawyers simply had grown old. While there was an enormous satisfaction in being able to achieve some sort of financial security for those injured children, the cost and drain on the lawyers had been enormous.

Is it worth it? Although my sanity often is challenged by friends and family, you bet it is! During the drudge times you curse to yourself, at first quietly under your breath, and later loudly to anyone who will listen. You are determined that at the end of the month you will start driving a bus for the local transit company. But the high points are certainly worth it, and you slowly back away from your own threats.

All in all, life as a litigator is a very personally rewarding one. As an associate practicing litigation you will work your fanny off preparing a case for trial, only to watch in horror as the partner in charge, never nearly as wise or knowledgeable as yourself, messes everything up by asking all the wrong questions. Later, as a partner, you will, of course, ask all of the right questions and wonder why your young associates can't prepare a case as well as you did. From both perspectives, it's hard and challenging work, but work well worth your best efforts.

IT'S A DONE DEAL
Business Practice

Gregory S. Feis

Whether it's putting together a multimillion-dollar initial public offering of stock, working on an acquisition of a major corporation, or negotiating contracts, Gregory S. Feis spells out what it feels like to be a deal maker. Less well understood than their colleagues in litigation, transaction-oriented business lawyers get the satisfaction of putting a deal together rather than taking it apart. Highlighting the day-to-day aspects of the practice, author Feis debunks the myth that litigators have more fun.

Most trial attorneys subscribe to the theory that in the world of law, litigators have more fun. Their courtroom tactics and antics are the stuff of popular legend. Transactional legal work (or "office practice," as litigators sometimes call it) does not have the same aura of glamour and romance in the public mind. After all, when was the last time you saw Perry Mason work for months on a multimillion-dollar initial public offering of stock or Michael Kuzak of "L.A. Law" close an acquisition of a major corporation?

The truth is that the life of a transaction-oriented business lawyer is at least as exciting, challenging, fast paced, and diverse as that of a litigator—it just does not lend itself to dramatization on television and the silver screen. To fully appreciate this, it helps to understand the kinds of work typically performed by a transactional lawyer, the advantages and disadvantages of transactional practice, and the types of skills and qualities desirable in such an attorney.

I should point out that, though this chapter focuses on life as a "deal maker," there is much more to the practice of business law than work on significant corporate and business transactions. An office practitioner

Gregory S. Feis has been practicing corporate law since his graduation from law school in 1981. He is currently an associate in the Washington, D.C., office of Morgan, Lewis & Bockius.

will usually also spend a large amount of time counseling corporate clients on their day-to-day operations and long-term business plans, drafting and negotiating contracts, and occasionally assisting clients in an attempt to hold a failing deal or other business relationship together in order to avoid litigation. So keep in mind that just as all litigation is not courtroom work, all office practice is not deal making.

Life as a deal maker in most law firms involves practice in one or both of two different (but often related) areas of transactional work: (1) mergers, acquisitions, and similar fundamental corporate transactions and (2) securities law, including public offerings, private placements, and regulatory compliance.

Mergers and Acquisitions Practice

A mergers and acquisitions practice can cover a wide variety of deals, from friendly, negotiated acquisitions of one company by another to hostile takeovers. These deals may be structured as the purchase of a target company's assets or stock or as a merger or consolidation of the target company and its suitor.

In a "friendly," or negotiated, acquisition or merger, junior attorneys are called upon to exercise sophisticated organizational and analytical skills and to prepare, analyze, and keep track of the voluminous documents involved in the deal. This is not the sort of thing they teach you in law school, unfortunately. Usually all material contracts of the acquired company will have to be gathered and screened by counsel for that company and reviewed and analyzed for their importance by counsel for the acquiring company. In addition, assets and liabilities, licenses, permits, real estate title issues, insurance, financial statements, employment and shareholder agreements, and a host of other matters and issues must be reviewed by counsel on both sides of the deal.

Also, the acquisition or merger agreement is almost never the only contract between the parties. Additional documents may include agreements to assign assets and assume liabilities, bills of sale, new employment or noncompetition agreements for the principals in the acquired company, promissory notes, security agreements, escrow agreements, articles of merger, and so forth. If the stock of the company to be acquired is publicly or widely held, it will also be necessary to prepare and distribute to the shareholders a proxy statement containing specific, detailed disclosures about the deal. This is required by law in preparation for a special meeting of shareholders to vote on the proposed transaction.

Lawyers in the first year or two of practice will typically prepare some or all of the closing and disclosure documents referred to above. This type of work gives new attorneys excellent exposure to and involvement in the "big picture" of the transaction, while simultaneously allowing them to hone their skills on a small part of it.

THE MISAPPLICATION OF CORPORATE LAW TO REAL LIFE

© 1985 by Michael Goodman

As you gain experience in this area of practice, you will be called upon to prepare and negotiate the acquisition agreement and close the deal. The buyer will want the acquisition agreement to include extensive representations and indemnifications from the seller; conversely, the seller will want to limit these provisions—and thus its potential liability—as much as possible. The lawyers are closely involved in these negotiations, and indeed if and when the principals reach an impasse on certain issues they often look to their lawyers to keep the deal from falling apart. In this role, lawyers have a great deal of room to be as creative as possible and to exercise their business instincts. A good transactional lawyer must see both sides of the transaction and suggest, analyze, and evaluate creative solutions that both sides can accept.

In a hostile takeover environment (such as the tender offer and proxy fights that have recently made the headlines), a firm's corporate attorneys usually work alongside the litigators in that same firm, regardless of which side the firm is representing. This approach allows the firm to proceed with a business-oriented strategy while preparing for or initiating litigation intended either to move the hostile takeover attempt forward or to stall it, depending on the objective.

This type of hostile takeover work is extremely demanding and requires tremendous amounts of time and effort. Usually a large number of attorneys on both sides of the transaction work around the clock over a relatively short period—sometimes only a few days—since the life or death of a corporation or the careers of its managers can be decided overnight. In some cases, attorneys involved in this type of battle have come up with novel ideas that have not only made their client a winner in the fight but also created a place for the attorney in the history and lore of the profession. Esoteric strategies such as the "poison pill" and the "golden parachute" have been developed by counsel, working closely with investment bankers and other takeover specialists.

In short, the mergers and acquisitions area of legal practice can be quite exhilarating, and you can be sure that when working on this type of deal you will not be bored.

Securities Practice

Another main area of law in which the deal makers toil is securities offerings. These securities may be common or preferred stock, bonds, debentures, warrants, or other instruments, and the attorney may represent either the issuer, whose securities will be sold in the offering, or the underwriter, who arranges and coordinates the sale. These securities offerings may be either public or private transactions.

Public offerings are to many securities lawyers the most exciting and interesting of all possible projects, in spite of the fact (or because of the fact) that the federal and state regulatory framework and the often large amount of money involved make public offerings highly complex processes. While some public offerings can become routine, conducting the initial public offering of the stock of a company involves hundreds if not thousands of hours of legal work, usually spread out among a team of lawyers over a three- to four-month period or even longer. Lawyers for the issuer and the underwriter work together to put together the offering prospectus, which is distributed to the public, and the registration statement, which comprises the prospectus and other required disclosure documents and is filed by the issuer for review by the various federal and state regulatory authorities.

A great deal of negotiation takes place in a public offering, usually centered on the sale price of the securities, the size of the offering, and the commissions that the underwriter will charge. Unlike litigation, this process is not a zero-sum game; in other words, all parties can to some extent come out ahead. The issuer wants to raise as large an amount of money as possible while retaining control of the corporation and the flexibility to raise additional money in the future. The underwriter wants the size and price of the offering to be set so that the securities will sell in the market in which they are offered. The underwriter also wants as large a commission as it can negotiate with the issuer.

There will often be a number of "all hands" meetings among the issuer, the underwriter, and their respective counsel, as well as accountants and other advisers, at which the prospectus and the terms of the offering will be negotiated. Once the parties are happy with the prospectus, the registration statement is filed with the Securities and Exchange Commission and the various state regulatory agencies for review. The final step in the process is responding to the comments of, and to some extent negotiating with, these regulatory agencies and obtaining clearance for the issue and distribution of the securities.

Work on a public offering is very detailed. It may require drafting the same provisions over and over again, each time making what seem like only slight improvements in an effort to perfect the document. Some lawyers consider this to be tedious work. Many deal makers, however, derive great satisfaction from producing a high-quality prospectus and successfully guiding the offering through the various phases and avoiding the various pitfalls.

Private placements of securities are similar to public offerings, but with fewer regulatory constraints and much more flexibility. In a private placement, a small number of investors who are usually fairly sophisticated and who are often somehow affiliated with the issuer form the sole market for the securities. Therefore, less disclosure is required than in public offerings, and the rules for sale and distribution of the securities are somewhat less stringent.

Is Deal Making for You?

To answer the question of whether you would enjoy doing corporate or securities work in the deal making area, begin with this understanding: as a deal maker, you may never in your career see the inside of a courtroom. So, if you have always dreamed of swaying a jury or dramatically finding a fatal flaw in an opponent's case, then transactional work is probably not for you.

However, if you enjoy work that allows for a high degree of creativity and the opportunity to work with lawyers representing other parties who are less than starkly adversarial, and if you enjoy negotiation and convincing other lawyers that your approach and your client's desires are reasonable, logical, and appropriate, then corporate and securities work may be for you.

There is another, somewhat more subtle difference between deal making and litigation. Litigation is by definition an adversarial process. The feeling of accomplishment at a postclosing celebration dinner is one that most litigators never experience.

Deal making (with the possible exception of hostile takeovers), on the other hand, is by nature usually a cooperative process of working with, rather than against, the other parties. By the time the lawyers become involved, the parties have generally reached an agreement to "do the deal." In short, the deal maker's challenge is to find creative ways around the tough points so that all parties concerned finally feel comfortable with the deal and the relationship that it has created.

Give life as a deal maker a try. Compared to your litigator colleagues, you may not see your practice on television as much, but the rewards and the challenges are all there.

HOME SWEET OFFICE
Law Firm Life

Cory M. Amron

Law firms aren't all alike, and they certainly aren't all like the one featured on "L.A. Law." Cory M. Amron, herself a partner in a major Washington, D.C., firm, explores the ways in which a law firm is a business and what that means for starting associates. Everything from the size of the firm to the types of clients it has to the way it bills them can affect the ambience. Highlighting the pitfalls to avoid, Amron provides a compelling and realistic view of law firm life.

Don't let anyone fool you. Law firms and lawyers are not all alike. Rather, firms are groups of individuals, each of whom has a different personality, a different perspective, and different expectations. Your life at one firm may not even resemble your friend's life at another.

The Law Firm as a Business

Law firms, whether they wish to view themselves as such or not, are essentially like any other businesses. Much like a company manufacturing widgets, the law firm must sell a product to support its employees (staff and associates), pay its overhead (rent, insurance, supplies), and provide to its owners (partners) a return (distributions) on their investment (capital). The law firm's product happens to be legal services, but like the widget company the firm must find a market (clients) for its products and bill its product at a competitive rate (legal fees) in order to survive and prosper (strive to satisfy all partners, associates, and staff with regard to their salaries, work, distributions, benefits, and amenities).

Cory M. Amron is a partner in a large Washington, D.C., law firm but started her legal career at a medium-sized firm that experienced growth gradually at first, and then precipitously through mergers. She is a graduate of Harvard Law School and has been active in the District of Columbia Bar, the local and ABA young lawyers groups, and the Women's Bar of the District of Columbia. She is an appointed member of the ABA's recently formed Commission on Women in the Profession.

Law firms have traditionally been organized as partnerships because state statutes forbade professionals, such as doctors and lawyers, from incorporating. Incorporation would have insulated the owners from liability for their professional conduct, and that was frowned upon. So the lawyers who started firms organized them as sole proprietorships or partnerships and hired employees (associates) to help them with the work. In addition, before a law school education became the most accepted method of training for the bar, associates would serve an apprenticeship, known as reading the law, at the office of an admitted bar member. In time, those associates were admitted to the bar, clamored for a piece of the ownership of the firm, and the partnership track was born.

Although modern statutes enable lawyers to incorporate their practices as professional corporations, the partner/associate dichotomy is still used to describe shareholders and legal employees, and the push for partnership (in this case an offer of shareholder status) continues to drive law firms.

Back to widgets. How do firms make their income, and what impact does that have on your life as a lawyer? Since the motive is to keep the firm running, income in a law firm must meet and, ideally, exceed expenses. In selling widgets, it is a matter of setting a price that covers costs, letting those who need widgets know that you make them, balancing quality against the price the market will bear, and rendering your sales service efficiently and in a manner to encourage repeat business.

In the legal business, the "price" of service can be (1) a predetermined dollar amount per hour times the number of hours spent on a matter (e.g., $50 per hour times 4 hours spent = $200), (2) a set fee for a specified service (e.g., $300 for all residential real estate settlements), (3) a contingency fee that is a percentage of money won for the client (and no money if the matter is lost) regardless of the time spent (e.g., 1/3 of the monetary award of $3,000 = $1,000), or (4) a combination of these methods. The first is the most prevalent billing arrangement. Contingency fees are charged by some litigators but are disfavored by larger firms because of the difficulty in budgeting income.

Regardless of the billing practices of your firm, as an associate or a partner you will be required to keep track daily of time spent on each client matter (in increments of 6, 10, or 15 minutes, depending upon firm procedure). This time is called "billable hours" and can vary from your actual clock-in/clock-out time by quite a bit. You could get to the office at 9 a.m. and leave at 6 p.m. yet only bill 7 of those 9 hours because of lunch, coffee breaks, work on pro bono, or other nonbillable matters.

At the end of a billing cycle, the firm compiles a report by computer of the time each attorney has billed to each client matter. If billing is done by hourly rates, the computer multiplies the time spent by each attorney's billing rate (which varies according to the attorney's experience) to calculate the bill for the client in that billing cycle. When the client pays the bill, the firm has received its income.

Law Firm Economics and You

Why is this analysis important? Because all the components of this process affect your life as a lawyer in a law firm. How many hours your firm expects you to bill will dictate how long your workday is and whether you must work evenings or weekends or both to meet expectations. For example, 1,800 billable hours a year are achievable by billing an average per day (although there is no such thing as an average day for a lawyer) of 8 billable hours, five days a week, and allowing for three to four weeks for vacation and holidays. Depending upon the type of work you do, the type of clients your firm has, and the billing policies of your firm, billing 8 hours could take you anywhere from 8 to 11 hours a day. The overriding message here is that life for an attorney at a law firm is almost *never* a 9-to-5 job and frequently requires evening and weekend work, especially at the associate level. Part-time positions are gaining acceptance but are still the exception rather than the rule.

The type of clients your firm has and the kinds of matters handled for them may dictate hourly rates and, consequently, how much can be made and paid for the attorney's work. Together with the pressures to pay competitive salaries, these factors will also affect your life.

Imagine hiring a large New York law firm to handle your house closing. After its lawyers have drafted and negotiated the contract, searched title, worked out practical problems, and attended the closing (which may take a few hours because of haggling), you receive a bill from the firm for 10 hours, which has been multiplied by a $175 per hour billing rate. You now owe $1,750 for this simple closing. Obviously, these types of client matters cannot be handled affordably by such a firm. If taken by a smaller firm that charges $50 an hour, that same matter would result in a $500 bill. But unless income is generated through a method other than hourly billing, or unless less-expensive paralegals handle more work, the economic consequences for the smaller firm may be lower salaries for the associates and offices located in a lower-rent district.

Although there seems to be a glut of lawyers these days, the most prestigious and larger firms continue to compete for attorneys. This competition has recently accelerated the increase in salaries for starting associates. Law school graduates in New York, for example, currently command an annual salary of more than $70,000 from large firms, an increase of more than 200 percent over starting salaries ten years ago. And, since no other lawyer in the firm wants to make less than the starting associates, the increases have a "trickle up" effect, ratcheting associates' salaries skyward. But look again at how income is generated. In many instances, it is the number of hours times the billing rate. Competition to keep clients usually discourages firms from increasing their billing rates, so billable-hour requirements must rise if the firm is to collect the income to meet its rising salary expenses. The effect on your life: in general, starting salaries that rise faster than billing rates usually mean longer hours at the office.

Clients

Clients are your firm's customers. If you have chosen a firm with an institutional base of clients (clients who come to the firm for services long after the original partner who introduced them to the firm is gone), life at that firm will differ substantially from a firm comprising attorneys with clients who are there *only* because of them. Time was (and not too long ago) when a firm's clientele was a stable commodity. Clients had longtime loyalties to firms and took their business elsewhere only under rare circumstances. Trends now are toward client hopping, splitting up legal work among a number of firms, or hiring in-house counsel to do work that outside counsel once handled.

The impact on your life: pleasing the client and keeping the bill within competitive bounds has become the focus of law firm attention. Short turnaround times, tight deadlines, and around-the-clock availability have become the norm. Once a leisurely and "gentlemanly" profession, the law now features attorneys who render legal services on their car phones during the commute to and from the office, who respond to beepers strapped to their waists, and who fear the phone on Friday afternoon lest it be that invaluable client calling with a Monday deadline.

In addition, attracting new business has become the lifeline of some firms. In the 1970s, the restraint on advertising by lawyers was lifted. Although most law firms do not advertise like your local car dealer, they do rely on partners to attract business and on all attorneys to hold and serve existing clientele.

How will these factors affect your life at a firm? Whether or not you will be expected to develop business as a partner (perhaps even as an associate) or just keep the existing clients satisfied may dictate the types of activities you pursue outside the office. And whether your personality is suited for such endeavors (or can be molded to fit them) may determine your satisfaction and success at a particular firm.

Super Support

Depending upon the size of a firm, support staff could be as small as one secretary or as large as a battery of word processors, secretaries, messengers, administrators, housekeeping personnel, and even chefs and chauffeurs. By and large, the quality of the support staff at private law firms cannot be duplicated in any other legal environment. Usually, an attorney shares a secretary only (if at all) with one other attorney, and these secretaries work harder to get the job done (and get paid substantially more) than secretaries in other types of businesses. The right secretary can help your life immeasurably. Your work product will look professional even if you would not otherwise know how to accomplish this, your efficiency can increase tenfold, your administrative burdens can be lifted, and you will easily negotiate the maze through which you must travel to get your written product from your head to your client's desk. If your success at your firm depends upon getting the job done whatever the hour and no matter how big the task, you are going to need this dedicated and competent support.

Type of Practice

Like clients, the type of practice of any particular firm depends upon, or is the sum of, what each attorney brings to the firm or retains for the firm. A firm does not magically attract a Federal Trade Commission or litigation practice by putting a notice in its window. Rather, clients come to a firm based upon the expertise and reputations of the attorneys at the firm.

Often you will find firms or departments within firms that are labeled as one type of practice but really handle either a wider variety of matters or a much narrower practice than one would expect. A tax department may be handling general corporate matters or it may be doing criminal tax fraud litigation. An international practice may be simply Federal Trade Commission work. An antitrust practice may have dried up and a firm or department turned toward general litigation. This, of course, will affect the type of work you do, so don't make assumptions from departmental or overall firm self-labeling. Many firms ultimately specialize only in what their clients bring to them.

Compensation

There is no doubt that law firms pay their associates and partners, on the average, much more than most other employers of legal talent. But there is a wide range of compensation between firms in the same city and between firms in different cities.

Be forewarned, however. The money has an allure that should not tempt those who do not have, or cannot develop, the personality for law firm life. Because people tend to live their lives at the highest level their incomes will allow, getting accustomed to a high salary at the beginning of your career may severely limit your options to change positions.

Small, Medium, or Large?

The size of a firm is relative and varies from city to city. As a guideline, however, small could be less than twenty, medium is about twenty to forty, and large is when your firm takes over more than one floor in the office building.

Smaller has some obvious advantages. Attorneys in small firms usually agree on philosophical matters: quality of life versus work hours, type of clients versus business to be turned away, and the style of management and direction of the firm. In short, the group may be more homogeneous and decisions made with each partner's input in a unanimous fashion. The firm may sport a family atmosphere, and everyone may know the cases or the types of matters others are handling. There may be more control and more independence. On the other hand, the work might not be varied, and the fate of the firm could rest on whether forces—economic or political—favor the type of practice in which the firm specializes.

From an associate's perspective, smaller firms pay more attention to each associate. Associates are not interchangeable, but, rather, intricate participants in the practice. Client contact is instantaneous and absolutely necessary, and each associate's work makes a tremendous difference to the firm.

The other side of this coin, however, is that small firms, especially overworked ones, may not have the luxury of training associates and oftentimes thrust them into the fray with minimal supervision. And some small firms are committed to their slow-growth policy—leaving little opportunity for additional partnership positions. But one thing is certain: a good associate in a small firm will never be stuck researching in the library or summarizing depositions.

Larger firms can afford more structured training programs, the work may be more sophisticated, and the remuneration may be higher. There may be opportunities to rotate through different practice groups before settling into one—thereby getting a taste of many areas of practice. A large practice can foot the bill for continuing legal education, bar association work, pro bono, and civic activities with greater ease than a small firm. More time may be available to discuss and set policies, and one may find more consistency in decisions made by large firms. An individual attorney in a large firm does not normally have to worry about administrative matters, since large firms usually have administrators, personnel directors, recruitment coordinators, librarians, and the like. Nonlegal tasks such as billing and accounting may also be handled by staff members.

But for some, the disadvantages of a large firm outweigh its advantages, leading them to avoid large firms or to change jobs after a few years. Associates tend to get lost in large firms. Unless one has a mentor, good work may go unsung and merit unrecognized. Unless a special effort is made, associates might not meet attorneys in other departments or obtain choice work assignments. Competition is more intense among associates as they perceive that not all of them will make it to partnership. Client contact, especially in the early years, may be limited. As previously mentioned, the hours may be longer.

Advancing to Partnership

The division of a law firm between partners and associates creates an expectation among new legal employees that they will be admitted to the partnership at some time in the future. But the path to partnership may be hazy at best, full of pitfalls at worst. The path is not the same for everyone; it may differ within sections of firms, and it may shift between the day you start and the day you are to be considered. If the ratio of partners to associates is an important factor in your firm and you come up for partner when few slots are available, you may not be admitted to the partnership.

© 1986 by Sam Hurt

In a recent study, it was found that young people first entering the job market believed that their hard work, dedication, and loyalty would determine the success of their careers. Political intrigue, mentors, and learning the rules and playing by them were thought to be unimportant. A word to the wise: skill and hard work will surely help, but don't underestimate those other factors.

The Myth of the Monolithic Law Firm

Many associates expect their firm to be consistent in its policies, its expectations, its treatment of associates, and the quality of its work. But this chapter began by characterizing a firm as a group of different people with differing personalities. This does not imply that firms do not have an overall atmosphere that you will either enjoy or loathe. When interviewing with firms in law school, I could sense a firm's working atmosphere just from sitting in the reception area. If everyone who walked by marched stiffly, heads up or down, and addressed each other as Mr. or Ms., I knew I could have walked out without interviewing. But if people used first names and greeted each other with warmth and a few jokes, I knew that firm had the collegiality I was looking for.

Maybe larger firms cannot be stereotyped by such reputations anymore, but the people with whom you work are often *more* important to your experience there than the type of work you do. The working style of one partner may drive you crazy, yet you may get on fabulously with the partner down the hall. Work that is rated as above average by one partner may be merely mediocre in the eyes of another. Do a super job for one partner, and your reputation may precede you and color each person's view of your work. More than you can imagine, the people who are your supervisors or become your mentors will influence the experiences you have, the types of matters you handle, your rate of learning and growth, and whether you make partner.

Is private law firm practice the right career track for you? Many law school graduates get drawn into this path of least resistance because firms bombard schools to recruit students. Consider law firm practice, assess yourself—your goals, life-style, and personality—and make an informed choice at the outset.

THE BOTTOM LINE
The Business of Law

Robert E. Bennett Jr.

The entire legal profession has experienced many changes during recent years, but none that threatens to ruin its very foundation as much as the shift from law as a profession to law as a business. Robert E. Bennett Jr., a partner in a Los Angeles law firm, explains the changes and their impact on what you can expect in your life as a lawyer.

At 14 I knew I wanted to be a lawyer. I had met only one attorney—my father's tennis partner. I thought a "tort" was a dessert (my favorite kind is Black Forest). I knew very little about the law.

Even if I had known more about practice, I never could have predicted the changes that would occur. During the last several years, the practice of law has shifted its emphasis from profession to business, becoming more profit oriented. In the "old days," before the 1980s, firms virtually ignored their role as businesses. They obtained new clients by referrals from satisfied clients and by long years of slowly building the reputation of the firm and its attorneys. Actual advertising for clients was unheard of. Today, some attorneys think nothing of making highly stylized television commercials, and there are law organizations with offices coast-to-coast in the many branch locations of huge retailers.

The long-range plans routinely drawn up by corporations for decades are only now becoming commonplace with law firms. Firms used to make rough estimates of their annual budgets and fly by the seat of their pants. Today, more firms are preparing annual budgets, instituting inventory controls, and adopting cost-cutting measures routinely employed by corporations for years.

Robert E. Bennett Jr. is a partner in Greenberg, Glusker, Fields, Claman & Machtinger in Los Angeles, California. He is a graduate of Duke School of Law, a past chair of the Taxation Section of the Los Angeles County Bar Association, and a fellow of the American College of Probate Counsel.

Office Management

Gone are the days when a partner had a secretary spending a fair amount of the day balancing the partner's checkbook, making travel plans, and setting up social engagements. Professional office managers have replaced more senior secretaries who tried to work in some administrative tasks around their attorneys' needs for secretarial assistance.

Executive directors, who function much like chief executive officers in corporations, are becoming commonplace in law firms. Most executive directors have a staff of two or three administrative types who supervise the support staff. The executive director, unlike the old office manager, is not only welcome at partners' meetings but is a necessary party at such meetings. Naturally enough, the executive director does not get involved in the practice of law and is well advised to stay out of recruiting and attorney compensation matters, but almost everything else is fair game. The concept of an executive director makes a lot of sense in the abstract, and the high qualifications and salary are often justified because otherwise an able partner or committee of partners is required to perform the same tasks with a corresponding loss of attorney time that could otherwise be devoted to billable client matters.

Billing

Attorneys work on particular projects for their clients and generally charge an hourly rate for the time spent on the project. The rate varies depending on the experience of the lawyer working on the matter. Attorneys record the client project and time spent each day on a time sheet.

Advanced technology has now arrived on the law firm scene, replacing time sheets recorded and cut manually, transformed into bills, and typed. Today there are many computer terminals on those fancy carved wooden desks, and billing, a once laborious process, has been streamlined. But even when monthly computer billing came into vogue, most firms regularly ran at least a month and often two months behind in the process. There were always attorneys who would not turn in their time sheets promptly, and this problem has not entirely disappeared. Computer-generated invoices can now be sent to all clients for the previous month as soon as the 9th or 10th, resulting in a return of a meaningful portion of the total sum billed before the end of the month.

Although hourly billing has always been the norm, some kinds of cases have traditionally been taken on a different kind of arrangement, known as a contingent fee. Attorneys are paid a percentage of the recovery, usually 25 to 33 percent, if they win the case. This fee arrangement is particularly common for attorneys who represent plaintiffs in personal injury cases.

Firms have now expanded their billing arrangements beyond these two traditional molds and are offering clients a variety of options. Clients may pay a flat fee for a particular service, or the hourly rate they are charged may be a single rate regardless of the experience of the attorney who works on the case. Attorneys are also offering a reduced hourly rate during the pendency of the case in exchange for a percentage of the recovery if they are successful, and some services that may take little time but require special expertise may be billed at a single flat amount without regard to hourly rate.

© 1984 by Michael Goodman

Loyalty

The shift to practice as a business has also spawned some other events virtually unknown in practice ten years ago. One of those is the dissolving firm. Traditionally, firms stayed in business. Names on law firm doors might change from time to time, but the same basic groups of people continued to practice together. Competitive pressures finally began to catch up with law firms in the early 1980s. Students who had chosen a particular firm as a "permanent" home arrived on the scene only to discover that the firm was in financial difficulty and was about to fold. Since then, the profession has seen even large firms with hundreds of attorneys close their doors or reorganize into two or more new firms.

Attorney loyalty to firms has also changed with the new emphasis on the profession as a business. Moving from one firm to another was a rare occurrence fifteen years ago; now legal recruiters, known as headhunters, make thousands of dollars finding new positions for young associates as well as for more seasoned attorneys with a substantial number of clients. This phenomenon, known as lateral hiring, has shifted the focus somewhat from the good of the firm or the "team" to the good of the individual attorney. If a better deal is offered down the street, it is likely to be accepted.

Recruiting

Recruiting new lawyers, too, has the taste of business. Before 1960, young law graduates seeking their first job had to "hit the bricks," hoping for an audience of a few minutes with a senior partner. Today, firms are constantly growing, and the addition of new legal talent from the law schools is an important element of this growth. Firms spend thousands of dollars in travel, entertainment, and attorney time to court law students who are at the top of their classes in well-respected law schools.

Running summer clerkship programs is even more expensive. While students use their summer clerkships to investigate the firm before accepting a permanent offer, firms are investigating the students, hoping to entice those who work out to return as full-time associates. Obviously, the more clerks who return as associates, the less firms must interview third-year students. The intense contact that a summer clerkship provides permits both the law student and the firm to make intelligent, fully informed decisions that will, hopefully, lead to a long-term, mutually satisfying and successful relationship culminating in partnership for the law student.

Partnership

Partnership, the brass ring of law firm life, has not escaped the tension between law as a profession and as a business. Law firms have always made it difficult for their associates to become partners. Traditionally, good work and staying power almost guaranteed partnership; however, competitive recruiting and profit orientation have changed the partnership model to "up or out." After six to ten years, associates are considered for partner. Those who are not chosen are on the street looking for new jobs. The few who make partner are those who play the game well and who for intangible and subjective reasons manage to attract favorable attention at the right time. There are firms today who are hiring as many as 100 people in a single class with no reason to expect more than 10 to make partner in six to ten years.

© 1982 by Sam Hurt

This partnership model has had a dramatic effect on the behavior of associates who want to be partners and on partners themselves. Bringing in business, billing an extremely large number of hours, and finding a way to collect for all or nearly all of those hours have increased in importance as attorneys today pay a great deal of attention to getting, keeping, and utilizing business. At luncheon clubs, on the golf course, in social settings, and at business, civic, and charitable activities, attorneys are seeking to make new and lucrative client contacts.

These ever-increasing pressures to produce clients, hours, and collections, as well as high-quality legal work, are leaving attorneys less time for other endeavors, including public service work. Although many firms still subsidize and encourage such work, whether it is working on a case for an indigent client or working on a bar association committee, the time for such activity is limited. Those attorneys who do find the time, however, find such work particularly satisfying. Thus, although business and competition are important and gaining in importance every day in the practice of law, attorneys continue to think of themselves as belonging to a collegial group, as being a part of a profession, and as marching to some higher ethical authority than their counterparts in the business world.

Given the general public image of attorneys, as reflected in the many current attorney jokes, one wonders whether they will continue to succeed in their efforts to run businesses while maintaining high ethics and principles. I have been at this profession for nearly twenty years, and while I am a realist and quite candid in my criticisms about the practice, I remain impressed by the lawyers I practice with and those I meet in negotiations and in the courts. There will continue to be a tension between the old style of practice and the need to be efficient and businesslike, but, for the present, the professional inside the businessperson is winning.

IN-HOUSE
Corporate Counsel

Roger A. Briney

Not all attorneys in the private sector work for law firms. Roger A. Briney outlines the job of corporate, or "in-house," counsel. Whether serving as a contact point between management and outside counsel or providing direct legal advice, the in-house lawyer can have the best of both worlds and have access to top management at the same time. Author Briney also explodes the myth that in-house corporate practice is sleepier and less lucrative than practice in a private law firm.

In recent years, the corporate perception of the role and function of in-house counsel has changed, and corporate law practice has been transformed from a relatively unchallenging, mundane existence, limited to "managing" legal work done by others, to a dynamic, challenging role that involves rendering legal advice on matters in virtually every area of the law and participating directly in management decision making on those matters.

There are essentially three levels at which a corporate legal department may handle individual legal issues confronting the corporation. The first is to have in-house counsel serve primarily as a contact point between management and outside counsel. Under this arrangement, the company's own lawyers seldom participate in ascertaining the merits of, or solutions to, legal problems. They simply determine which outside counsel are best suited to handle the problem and then manage that firm's representation. The second is to rely exclusively on in-house counsel for legal advice or representation in legal proceedings. Finally, a hybrid of these two approaches may be applied to a particular legal issue.

Roger A. Briney has worked as both a business executive and a lawyer for American Telephone & Telegraph and currently practices in the Fairfax, Virginia, office. He is a 1975 graduate of the University of Georgia and chaired the YLD's Committee on Public Utility Law in 1988–89.

Evolution of Corporate Practice

Historically, in-house corporate practice was largely limited to the first of these alternatives. Corporations perceived outside lawyers as a necessary evil and employed in-house counsel to manage their relations with law firms that represented the corporation. Legal staffs at corporations were generally very small, and corporate counsel were generalists. The lack of direct involvement in specific legal issues removed many of the pressures and demands generally associated with law practice. Because this type of involvement primarily required resource management skills, rather than legal acumen, corporate counsel positions were viewed as less satisfying and prestigious than those in private practice.

With rising costs of legal representation caused by both inflation and the dramatic surge in the degree of government regulation of corporate affairs during the 1970s, many corporations had to reevaluate their needs for legal advice and representation. After comparing the hourly fees charged by outside counsel (often close to $200 per hour) with the costs of employing in-house counsel, corporations realized that substantial savings could be achieved by expanding the size of law departments and assigning work in-house. Furthermore, with corporations becoming involved in an ever-expanding array of legal issues, efficiencies could be achieved by using in-house counsel familiar with the nature of the business, its technology and terminology, the resource and contact persons involved, and any other important background information relevant to a particular issue.

Of course, no two corporate legal departments are the same. The mix of hands-on legal work versus management of outside counsel varies greatly and often depends on the complexity of the legal issue and the availability and capability of in-house counsel to address the issue. Today, even when work is "farmed out," in-house counsel frequently act as partners in developing solutions to legal problems or representing the corporation in litigation. In such situations, in-house counsel generally are more familiar with the operations of the corporation, the sources of necessary factual information, and the key personnel involved. Outside counsel rely on access to this kind of information to fashion optimum solutions or strategies.

Corporations in the telecommunications, pharmaceutical, computer, and automobile industries, among others, have long relied on in-house counsel to perform legal work, particularly in specialized areas of the law such as labor relations, patents, and state and federal regulatory matters. Because all of these specialties require extensive knowledge of a particular industry, not to mention the operations of a particular company, and because of the volumes of legal work in these areas, it has always made sense to develop that expertise in-house.

Lawyers in Corporate Practice

To meet these needs, many corporate employers hire lawyers with vary-ing backgrounds. Most have had a number of years' experience in par-ticular fields of law working for either law firms or the government, al-though corporations also hire recent graduates for entry-level positions. This mix brings a diversity of experience and business knowledge that permits a corporation to rely heavily on the participation of its attorneys in day-to-day decision making.

Although my career is certainly not typical among in-house attorneys, it may provide some insight into some of the possible functions and re-sponsibilities of corporate counsel. After graduation from law school in 1975, I was employed by a major corporation as a manager responsible for developing the prices for services and defending those prices before a federal regulatory commission. This involved developing rate plans, preparing documentation to support those plans, answering interroga-tories, and preparing drafts of various pleadings.

© 1988 by Sam Hurt

After three years as a manager, I became an attorney in the company's legal department. My responsibilities were varied and included review-ing and negotiating contracts, providing advice and defending the com-pany in litigation on antitrust and employee benefit matters, preparing resolutions for action by the board of directors, and providing advice on marketing issues. Some of these functions were fascinating—the anti-trust counseling and marketing advice required extensive research and application of that research to specific alternatives being considered by the corporation. I participated in deliberations leading to decisions of importance not only to the company but also to the industry as a whole. Other functions were often tedious and mundane—for example, review-ing contract after contract and examining millions of pages of docu-ments that would ultimately be produced to plaintiffs in numerous anti-trust suits. Probably no attorney is enamored with all of the work that must be done. However, unlike private practitioners, I found that I could use these mundane assignments to gain additional insights into our business that proved valuable in subsequent assignments.

As time passed, my involvement in antitrust litigation increased. Because of the knowledge gained as a former manager, and through my review of countless documents, I was placed on the trial team defending the company in a major government antitrust suit. Outside counsel and I jointly participated in six months of negotiations with Department of Justice lawyers to hammer out a set of stipulations (agreed facts) and a statement of contentions that would govern the conduct of the trial. I assisted several witnesses in the preparation of prefiled written testimony, prepared them for cross-examination, and presented them at trial. I also provided cross-examination material to lead counsel and other attorneys assigned to cross-examine government witnesses. Through this assignment, I enhanced my litigation and negotiation skills and acquired still more insight into the company's business.

Challenges v. Safety

Historically, corporate practice was perceived as "safe," but not necessarily lucrative. If one joined a corporate law department it was generally believed that, although much of the wealth and prestige of private law practice were forgone, one gained stability and job security and was subject to less onerous work. This is less and less true for many corporate counsel. Many lawyers have been faced with changes in employers or responsibilities because of changes in the identity of their corporate clients caused by reorganization, divestitures, mergers, or acquisitions. In these circumstances, some corporate counsel may find that their skills are no longer needed. But these kinds of changes also bring opportunities. Those with skills and knowledge valuable to the new organization frequently find their careers enhanced. In mergers or acquisitions, attorneys from an acquired entity can provide invaluable assistance in achieving integration of the two organizations.

I was involved in such a corporate reorganization, and my responsibilities have changed significantly. Rather than focusing on historical events in which the corporation was involved, as one does frequently in antitrust litigation, I became a staff attorney providing advice to headquarters clients on state regulatory matters. I also helped create and disseminate corporate policy to regional attorneys who practice before state regulatory agencies. Today, *I* am one of the regional attorneys appearing before state regulatory agencies. My coworkers and I together formulate litigation strategy and prosecute state regulatory cases.

Most corporations with large legal staffs have diverse interests and can provide opportunities for in-house attorneys to pursue practice in virtually every area of the law. Indeed, many encourage attorneys to move from one discipline to another, from one subsidiary or division to another, and from one geographical location to another so that individual attorneys can gain a better understanding of all facets of the business.

Unlike my friends in private practice, I frequently become involved in legal issues long before they surface as legal problems. In my position as in-house counsel, I have the opportunity to provide preventive advice, allowing my clients to avoid or minimize risks. I participate directly in management decision making, rather than as outside counsel simply providing advice. Because my clients are more often than not also friends, I enjoy strong working relationships that are often nonexistent between outside counsel and corporate clients. Although I am involved only in issues affecting my company, that company is large and diverse, and there are virtually no limits on the variety of legal issues I may address. I am expected to be a lawyer and not simply a contact or manager of outside counsel. As a result, my practice is neither mundane nor repetitious but rather is diverse and stimulating. With these expectations—like lawyers in private practice—I must frequently work long hours to meet deadlines caused by demanding schedules and my own standards.

While I may never reap monetary rewards comparable to those that a few obtain in private practice, the challenges associated with being a member of a corporate management team and influencing its success in the marketplace can provide more personal satisfaction and lasting friendships.

FOR THE PEOPLE
Government Practice

David B. Kopel

Lawyers are practicing at every level of government, representing the general public welfare in one sense or another. David B. Kopel explores factors such as the desire to "do good" for the public, personal life-style preferences, and the opportunity for hands-on training and advancement, all of which should be considered in deciding whether or not a government practice is right for you.

A legal career in government practice can be a challenging and rewarding alternative to joining a law firm after graduation. The opportunities for legal employment in the public sector are much more varied than the roles of public prosecutor and public defender with which we have become familiar through popular television drama over the years. Lawyers are found working at all levels of government: federal, state, county, city, and even specialized entities such as water authorities, taxing entities, and government corporations. The numerous types of public legal employment available and the varied areas of law with which government attorneys deal offer the young attorney an interesting practice that also provides unique opportunities to gain practical experience and substantive knowledge and the satisfaction of serving the public.

Many Flavors

An attorney considering a public-sector practice can find work associated with any of the three branches of government. For example, both the U.S. Congress and the federal court system employ lawyers as re-

David B. Kopel is currently an Assistant Attorney General in the Hazardous Waste Unit of the Natural Resources Division of the Colorado State Attorney General. He has also worked as an assistant district attorney in Manhattan. He notes that New York City has more crime than Colorado has hazardous waste.

searchers and as clerks. Some attorneys are hired to draft and review legislation. The armed services employ thousands of lawyers, both military and civilian, to perform the myriad legal tasks that those large organizations and their personnel require. The Department of Justice hires many attorneys to handle routine litigation and courtroom business or to serve in special units that oversee the most complex and specialized litigation and legal business facing the United States. Additionally, many, if not all, federal agencies have a legal staff to address problems faced in the course of day-to-day regulatory activities, and some have a corps of administrative law judges to hear and propose decisions in contested cases.

Except military positions and those legal jobs that involve such specialized functions as the conduct of foreign relations and other peculiarly federal areas of interest, this hierarchy of lawyers, somewhat reduced in size and numbers, is duplicated in state governments. Most states have administrative agencies that have legal staffs and administrative law judges. Offices of state attorneys general represent the state government and are often charged with enforcing certain consumer and civil rights. In many states, the public defender system is an arm of the government.

Local governments, especially large cities, also require lawyers' services. County attorneys or district attorneys prosecute criminals. City attorneys and attorneys on their staffs may draft ordinances, oversee regulatory functions such as enforcement of building codes and zoning restrictions, oversee the provision of utility services, and represent the city in litigation.

Government law practice is exceedingly varied in its substantive scope as well. The variety of areas of law open to government attorneys is as broad as that available in private practice. Government attorneys who prosecute criminal offenses may do so under antitrust legislation, drug enforcement laws, internal revenue code provisions, or innumerable other statutes. Many government lawyers are happy to practice as business lawyers rather than litigators. Their duties may include licensing health facilities or radio broadcasting companies, drafting environmental regulations, or administering welfare laws. Virtually every aspect of law practice open to the private practitioner—contract litigation, securities, tort defense, real property law, taxation, administrative law, environmental law, criminal law—has an analogue in government practice.

Who's the Client?

Perhaps the most interesting distinction between private and public practice has to do with the matter of clients. Many government legal positions do not involve a significant amount of client contact. It may be difficult, for example, as a lawyer for an administrative agency, to even identify a particular client. In other cases, such as that of a prosecutor or city attorney, the client is a more nebulous conglomeration of persons natural and artificial: "the United States," "the People of the State of Montana," or "the City of St. Louis." On the one hand, a most rewarding aspect of the practice of law is the special relationship that can bind attorneys and their clients, and some government lawyers miss out on this. On the other hand, the lack of individual client responsibility can be a blessing.

In a nutshell, service to individual clients can be the heart and soul of law practice, or it can be a pain in the neck. In the private sector, stories are easy to come by about clients calling lawyers at home at the most inopportune times and with the most bizarre questions. A private practitioner may feel forced, for obvious reasons, to be pleasant to some paying clients who are very unpleasant people. Although any prosecutor, city attorney, or administrative agency lawyer can tell you that crime victims and taxpayers often do not seem as grateful as one might hope, nonetheless, these government lawyers find great personal satisfaction in sending a dangerous criminal to jail, defending a city from a frivolous lawsuit, or exercising the right of the government to prohibit the discharge of toxic wastes into the environment, all in the service of their public "client."

Good News, Bad News

As with most career choices, there are advantages and disadvantages to consider in choosing employment as a government attorney. For some, work as a government attorney is a chance to fulfill a strongly felt desire to serve the public. Some law schools ask prospective students to write short essays describing why they have applied for admission. Many applicants write about the opportunity to make society better through their hoped-for legal career. Unfortunately for these noble souls, positions as lawyers for "white knight" public interest organizations such as the Environmental Defense Fund or the American Civil Liberties Union are very difficult to get, and those positions that are available often go to lawyers with several years' experience. For this reason, law school graduates who want to "do good" in their work can often meet this goal through working in the public sector.

Government lawyers, as much as their colleagues in public interest jobs, are paid to practice law *pro bono publico*. Translated from Latin, this means "for the public good." Like all law practice, however, government practice can also require the performance of work that lawyers may find morally unappealing, such as enforcing an unpopular law or defending

79

an action that they cannot condone personally. Within boundaries, the young government lawyer may, however, have the discretion to choose which cases to press most vigorously and which to compromise. Some government positions (especially in the criminal justice system) will expose the lawyer to the seamier side of life and society. While such exposure means that the job will never be dull, and dealing with such diverse elements can lead to a certain poise and ability to deal with almost any situation, lawyers choosing to serve in such positions must be prepared to guard themselves against disillusionment and eventual burnout. While young government lawyers, like young private practitioners, will do their share of tedious and perhaps unpleasant work, government lawyers may find such work more rewarding in the knowledge that their work, in some way, contributes to the greater welfare of the public.

© 1983 by Michael Goodman

"Pssst, Your Honor, not meaning to complain, but I foresee a potential conflict of interest with my court-appointed counsel."

Some people who choose public law practice do so for more personal reasons. While, as a rule, most government attorneys carry heavy workloads, they are more or less free from the constraints of billable hour goals that govern so much of the professional lives of their colleagues in private practice, and they may really get to take vacations. While not all government lawyers go home at 5:30, most do lead a more humane lifestyle than private practitioners. A government lawyer may work several weekends before a trial, but nobody will call with a rush assignment the day before Thanksgiving. Government lawyers are also relieved of business development pressures. For lawyers in private practice, particularly with small firms, success depends largely on one's ability to network with clients and potential clients and to play the "rainmaker."

The advantage of more reasonable working hours and less pressure to develop a clientele does not come without a price. Government lawyers' salaries are generally far lower than those of their private practice counterparts. In fact, salaries may be as little as 20 to 50 percent of salaries in private practice positions in major cities. Even if the starting pay is competitive for the area where the new government lawyer works, it will probably increase on a fixed scale and peak relatively early. While the pinnacle of the corporate legal world is the corner office, in government work one may be lucky to get the corner of an office. Especially in the first few years, government lawyers may have tiny desks and may have to type. The support network on which private law firms rely is limited or nonexistent. Messengers and paralegals tend to be the exception rather than the rule.

Sometimes, because these factors may make government practice unattractive to many top law school graduates, there may also be a loss of status associated with certain lower-level government legal jobs. However, experienced government attorneys may advance to very prestigious positions that include management responsibilities, such as section leader within a state attorney general's office or even general counsel or chief administrative law judge for an administrative agency. Others may find that even a few years of experience in a government position opens the door to more highly paid jobs in the private sector.

Government law practice provides excellent training for those who can handle the extra responsibility it entails. A government law office cannot afford the luxury of providing systematic training for a new lawyer, which may be both an advantage and a disadvantage. Although big law firms may promise you excellent training, government positions generally provide more "learning by doing" earlier in your career. This is especially true for those who are interested in litigation. Good litigation skills are developed more quickly from handling many small trials by yourself (or with limited supervision) for three years than from watching a senior law firm member handle one or two cases a year for a similar amount of time. While not everyone is suited for this sink-or-swim method of training, accelerated case responsibility can bring a great deal of early and satisfying career growth. Ex-prosecutors, ex–public defenders, and former assistant attorneys general are sought out for their abilities as seasoned trial advocates.

Government jobs that do not involve trial practice may also allow more responsibility earlier than that afforded associates in large law firms. Responsibility in such positions can be coupled with the opportunity to gain expertise in a substantive area of law. For example, an attorney serving as a staff lawyer or administrative law judge for an environmental agency or public utility commission or as an attorney for the planning department of a city will gain an invaluable understanding of the law of that particular area. Needless to say, many excellent tax lawyers started with the Internal Revenue Service, and up-and-coming securities lawyers vie for jobs with the Securities and Exchange Commission. Ex–military lawyers who specialized in government contracting and procurement can find their services in demand by defense contractors and others seeking business with the federal government. This combination of early responsibility and the development of substantive expertise makes a few years spent as a government lawyer a valuable credential.

The opportunities available in government practice are widely varied and certainly hold something of interest for almost everyone. However, upon careful consideration of the advantages and disadvantages of public practice, working for the government will not appeal to everyone. Whether attorneys who choose government positions do so initially from a desire to serve the public or from a personal life-style decision, and whether they stay with the government for only a few years or make government practice a career, a special job satisfaction will come from knowing that the work performed while there contributed to the good of the public. The lawyer who can rise to the unique challenges of government practice will find rich rewards for hard work, not least of which is the superior opportunity to "do well by doing good."

THE GOOD GUYS
Public Interest Advocacy

Elizabeth Symonds

The opportunity to advocate for a more humane and just society—be it in the arena of animal liberation or children's rights—is the privilege and challenge of those lawyers working in public interest law. Elizabeth Symonds writes from personal experience about the up side (furthering strong principles and beliefs) and the down side (low pay, minimal resources) of pursuing the path of public advocacy. Highlighting the frustrations and the excitement of representing those traditionally unrepresented or underrepresented in our society, Symonds makes a compelling argument for public interest law as a fulfilling career choice.

Attending a hospital bedside hearing where a judge has been asked to decide whether a cesarean section operation should be performed on a pregnant cancer patient; sitting at the counsel table at the U.S. Supreme Court, assisting at a death penalty case hearing; appearing on television and radio to address civil liberties topics such as strip searches of employees, drug testing in the workplace, and youth curfews. These are some of the opportunities and challenges of practicing public interest law. It's the kind of job that always keeps you busy and has a built-in guarantee that there will never be a dull moment.

Public interest attorneys advocate for individuals and groups who are traditionally unrepresented and underrepresented in our legal system. Since public interest lawyers generally charge little or no fee for their services, their clients are people who otherwise would be unable to afford representation. These might include prisoners, migrant farm workers, children, psychiatric patients, or immigrants.

Elizabeth Symonds has been a staff attorney since 1981 with the American Civil Liberties Union of the National Capital Area. She also spent a year as a graduate fellow of the Institute for Public Representation of the Georgetown University Law Center, a public interest law clinic.

The practice of public interest law is as exciting as it is diverse—covering a broad range of opportunities, from representing small advocacy groups dedicated to protecting consumer interests, furthering women's rights, or saving the whales to representing indigents involved in landlord-tenant disputes or domestic relations cases. The criminal public defender, paid by the government to represent indigents, represents yet another kind of public interest law.

Other government jobs can be classified in the public interest category. Some divisions within offices of state attorneys general specialize in consumer protection or civil rights law. Many local, state, and federal offices employ attorneys to monitor and implement fair employment and housing laws. The federal government's Department of Justice has an entire division dedicated to civil rights law.

Public interest jobs can be divided into two distinct categories: "service" and "impact." Service work is done by attorneys who help individuals with personal problems—indigents facing evictions, mothers on welfare about to lose their benefits, battered women seeking protection. Impact work involves litigation brought not only on behalf of a particular client, but with a view toward setting legal precedents that will affect many people. This might involve, for example, a case on behalf of an individual psychiatric patient in which a judge issues a broad ruling that psychiatric patients not be forced to submit to certain forms of treatment.

This Is Not a Law Firm

With this initial understanding of what public interest law is all about, we may take a closer look inside the office of a typical public interest lawyer. The day-to-day routine involves interviewing clients, performing legal research, writing briefs, appearing in court, and lobbying Congress and state legislatures—a practice strikingly similar to that of more traditional attorneys. Within the public interest field, job duties may vary, but the primary difference between the public interest attorney and the attorney engaged in a more traditional private practice is that the public interest attorney advocates not only for an individual client, but also to further the goal of a broad legal policy. Activities might include advocating for the rights of children to proper foster care or arguing for a legal precedent that will open doors for women to work in jobs previously closed because of sex discrimination.

Unlike private firms, which sometimes make decisions about the composition of their client base or the type of tasks they will perform based on potential profit, public interest attorneys typically do not select their cases or design their law practices based on financial considerations. Public interest law firms certainly have budgetary constraints (many have chronic financial problems), but they somehow manage to keep their goals in clear sight, rather than viewing their legal work as a means of making a profit.

Funding for public interest firms or groups varies widely. Some receive grants from foundations (in fact, the Ford Foundation initially funded many public interest organizations); others receive government funds. Some are membership organizations with a dues-paying structure. Many employ fund-raising methods, such as direct mail and telemarketing, to add to their financial resources. Court-awarded attorneys' fees, whereby a judge orders an opponent to pay the prevailing party's legal fees, are becoming an important source of income to these groups.

The pros and cons of entering this field vary widely, depending on the particular type of public interest office and on the needs and personality of the individual attorney. For many lawyers, public interest work presents an opportunity to get hands-on experience at an early stage in their legal careers. Because many public interest organizations are relatively small, attorneys must perform a variety of tasks—including court appearances—and often take primary responsibility for their own caseloads. This contrasts with the experience of some lawyers in very large private firms, who for the first several years out of law school perform legal research and writing tasks and share responsibilities for cases with other lawyers.

Ups and Downs

The major reason lawyers choose public interest law is the desire to use their legal skills to further a philosophical or political goal. Whether the immediate goal is saving endangered whales, establishing equal employment rights for disabled individuals, preserving a political group's right of free expression, or winning a damages award for a group of consumers cheated by a large corporation, there is a sense of great satisfaction in knowing that you are actually getting paid to work toward achieving personal political objectives.

The down side of public interest law may be summed up in one word: money. While some public interest groups are well funded, and many government public interest jobs have a strong financial base, most public interest organizations are constantly struggling to stay in the black. This translates into salaries that are less than those of most attorneys who enter private practice. In fact, public interest salaries, even for experienced attorneys, are almost universally lower than starting salaries paid by the nation's top firms. This can work a hardship on the young lawyer who faces repayment of college and law school loans. Although public interest lawyers may earn less than their law school classmates, their salaries are comparable to those received by professionals in other fields. Public interest salaries are certainly not at the starvation level!

Lack of funding can affect more than staff salaries. Public interest offices run on a relatively restricted budget and are often a little more cluttered and less well furnished than private law firms. And because of a lack of financial resources, public interest lawyers may have less access to legal computer systems, well-stocked law libraries, paralegal and support staff assistance, formal training programs, and litigation expenses (for filing fees, deposition costs, payment to expert witnesses, etc.) than do other private-sector lawyers.

Finding Your Niche

Despite the lower salary scales, finding a legal position in this field is more difficult than in many other areas of legal practice. This is primarily because budget constraints in public interest firms mean that fewer resources can be allocated to hiring attorneys; thus, fewer slots are available. In addition, there are fewer public interest firms and organizations than private law offices.

Also, public interest firms may not be well represented at law school placement offices, due in part to a lesser need to recruit new lawyers or expand their legal staffs and a general lack of funds in the budget for recruiting. This means that students interested in pursuing this field will probably not have the luxury of interviews at their law schools and travel expenses for out-of-town interviews. Students, rather, must use a great deal of initiative in identifying and applying for public interest jobs.

Many law students claim that they would choose a public interest career except for the fact that "there are no public interest jobs available." Although it may appear that way, especially compared to the hundreds of listings for commercial legal jobs, it simply isn't true. The jobs are there—it just requires a little more assertiveness and motivation to obtain them.

One way to accomplish this is to try to enter the public interest "network" early in your school career. This can be done even as an undergraduate. Working as an intern in a public defender's office or an environmental law firm can give you a taste for what the practice is like, help you meet people who might be helpful in your job hunt, and show future public interest employers that you have demonstrated a consistent commitment to the field.

This is even more important during law school. If you can get a summer clerkship with a public interest office or do a public interest internship for credit during the school year, this will provide you with invaluable experience for your future job hunt.

Unfortunately, not everyone has the financial resources to take these relatively low-paying types of jobs while they are students. But if you can, or if you can afford to serve as a volunteer with a public interest group, you might think of it as an investment toward a future public interest job.

Law schools are becoming more cognizant of the needs of students who want to enter the public interest field. Several law student and alumni groups have formed law foundations, based at various law schools, that are designed to help correct the perpetual funding problems in the field. Students and lawyers in these groups generally work for commercial firms but pledge a small percentage of their salaries to the foundation, which then gives grants to lawyers who want to create public interest projects. The foundation may give grants for summer public interest projects to law students at the particular school.

© 1988 by Michael Goodman

Other law schools provide fellowships to students who have a proven track record of service in the field and who will probably continue a public interest career after law school. A few schools are starting loan forgiveness programs, in which law graduates who work at public interest jobs repay their student loans at an initially lower rate and, if they remain in the field, eventually have some of the payments excused.

Almost any law school will provide a student with the essential skills needed to become a good public interest attorney. Public interest employers are as interested in good legal research and writing skills and sharp legal analytic ability as are commercial employers. If you are looking for an academic environment particularly hospitable to future public interest lawyers, you might do some research to determine which schools have these types of law foundations, fellowships, and loan forgiveness programs. You also might ask about the school's placement efforts in the public interest field, possibilities for public interest internships for academic credit, and law school clinic options, which often provide excellent hands-on experience for law students.

Public interest law is a challenging, exciting field, sometimes frustrating, often extraordinarily satisfying. It certainly is not for everyone, but for those seeking to merge legal skills and career choice with their personal principles aimed toward a more humane and just society, public interest law is a fulfilling option within the legal profession.

NOT ANOTHER KINGSFIELD
Teaching Law

Barbara E. Bergman

Few former law students will ever forget the first person who taught them that a tort was not a Black Forest cake. Barbara E. Bergman took her legal education back to the classroom as a law school professor. For Ms. Bergman, teaching law allows her to enjoy the gratification of working with students and the time to pursue her own intellectual interests in the law.

If three years in a classroom as a student isn't enough, consider becoming a law school professor. That thought may conjure up images of teaching class for a few hours a week and then taking long vacations during spring and summer breaks and grading examinations while lounging on a tropical beach drinking banana daiquiris. Unfortunately, that is not quite the reality, although many times I wish it were.

Qualifications for Teaching

Accept, for the moment, my assessment that it takes a great deal of work to be a good law professor. Assuming that you still want to pursue a teaching career, you need to spend some time determining whether you can get the kind of teaching position you would like. Finding a teaching job that you want these days is not as easy as you might expect. Having been through this type of selection procedure fairly recently, I was amazed at how little I actually knew about the process. Having survived, I can offer with the voice of experience the following suggestions to those interested in exploring the possibilities.

Barbara E. Bergman has worked as a public defender and private practitioner in the District of Columbia. She has been teaching criminal justice courses and clinical classes at the University of New Mexico School of Law in Albuquerque, New Mexico, since 1987 and taught juvenile law as an adjunct professor at Catholic University in Washington, D.C., for seven years. She is a graduate of Stanford University Law School and clerked for a judge in the Ninth Circuit Court of Appeals.

First, you need to appraise honestly the likelihood that you can get the kind of teaching position you want. Competition for law school teaching slots is stiff. One commentator recently estimated that there are approximately 1,000 applicants for about 125 open teaching jobs each year (Paul A. LeBel, "A Guide for the Selection of Faculty Recruiters," *Journal of Legal Education,* 1987, 37:374).

As premature as it may sound, it is helpful to know even before starting law school what qualifications often are required of law school teaching applicants. The caliber of law school from which you graduate as well as references from your law school professors may be important once you start looking for a teaching position. Most law school hiring committees, and ultimately the entire faculty, will be interested in your academic record as a law student even years after you graduate. They will want to know if you were on the law review and what, if any, honors you received. Having had a judicial clerkship after graduating is also considered a plus in the hiring process—depending upon the court and judge for whom you clerked. Because academia emphasizes research and writing, having a publication record is helpful in convincing a faculty that you have the potential to become a legal scholar. Finally, many schools will want to know why you are interested in teaching and whether you have taught before. If you have, they may want to see your evaluations and may request references from the school where you taught.

Finding a Teaching Position

The procedure through which most aspiring law school teachers actually apply for faculty positions is fairly organized and regimented. The Association of American Law Schools (AALS) serves as a coordinating center for teaching applicants and law schools with faculty openings. For a modest administrative fee, an applicant can fill out a one-page form listing legal education, publications, experience, and areas of teaching interest. These one-page resumes are then made available to law schools by the AALS. The AALS also distributes a placement newsletter, describing the various openings at law schools throughout the nation, to individuals who have submitted resumes and paid the fee.

The AALS sponsors an annual recruiting conference, which is usually held in November. Schools may contact individuals whose one-page resumes interest them in advance to schedule interviews at the conference. This recruiting conference provides a unique opportunity for applicants to interview with a variety of schools in one location. After the conference, the schools will invite those applicants in whom they are still interested for on-campus interviews. Interviews usually last for an entire day, if not longer, and some of the schools request that the applicant make a presentation to the faculty. (For additional details about this entire process, you may contact the AALS, Suite 370, One Dupont Circle, NW, Washington, D.C. 20036.)

In addition to, or instead of, this formal procedure for seeking a law school teaching position, you can contact the schools in which you are interested directly by sending an application letter and a resume to the dean or the chairperson of the faculty hiring committee. Professors at the law school from which you graduate may also be able to give you suggestions about schools and openings. If you are seriously pursuing an academic career and have additional questions, I recommend reading the following law journal articles: "So You Want to Be a Law Professor?" by E. Zenoff and J. Barron, *Journal of Law and Education*, 1983, 12:379, and "The Law Faculty Hiring Process," by J. Bruce and M. Swygert, *Houston Law Review*, 1981, 18:215.

Evaluating Teaching Positions

The next step in considering a career in the classroom is deciding what kind of teaching position to seek. There is a basic dichotomy at many law schools between an academic teaching slot and a clinical position. Clinical faculty members usually teach only in the clinical programs at law schools and do not teach traditional academic/substantive courses. Clinics typically involve practical experience for students representing either real or mock clients under the supervision of the faculty. The emphasis in such courses is on practical problems and drafting assignments that often arise in the actual practice of law, as compared to the typical lecture or discussion format of many law school classes.

An academic position, on the other hand, is usually devoted to instruction in the traditional law school classroom setting, with the emphasis on lectures and in-depth research and writing exercises. Although academic positions are oftentimes hectic in their own way, the hope is that the academician will have more time to think about issues and to work on longer-term projects than someone who is, in essence, a teacher/practitioner.

The distinction between clinical and academic faculty is a subject of controversy at many law schools throughout the country. The clinical faculty is viewed differently than the academic faculty at some schools. I am fortunate to have found a teaching position at one of the few schools that have totally integrated academic and clinical faculty; however, most law schools still struggle with this issue. If you are interested in a clinical position, you should find out exactly how clinical faculty members are treated at the schools where you would like to teach. You should ask about the following:

1. Are clinical faculty members on the normal tenure track, or are they treated as short-term or long-term contract employees?

2. If clinical faculty members are on the normal tenure track, are they expected to meet the same writing and publishing requirements as those in academic positions? This is an important consideration because most clinical jobs are so labor-intensive and time-consuming that it is difficult, if not impossible, to be a good clinical professor while also researching and writing high-quality legal articles.

3. If the clinical position is not a tenure-track slot, what are the terms of the contracts, and what is the likelihood that the contracts will be renewed regularly?

4. What is the expected work load for a clinical position? For example, how many students is each professor expected to supervise, and how many and what kind of cases is each student expected to handle?

5. Finally, how are clinical professors viewed by the academic faculty, and what, if any, rights do clinical instructors have vis-à-vis the other faculty members? At some schools, clinicians are viewed as second-class faculty members; they are not paid as much, and they may not be permitted to vote at faculty meetings on faculty hiring decisions or other issues affecting the law school.

Once you have decided what kind of teaching position interests you most, there is another list of items you should consider. As obvious as it may sound, you should think about where you want to live. Often family obligations or simple personal preference may limit the locations you consider. This may not create any difficulty if you have no such restrictions or happen to be looking in an area with numerous law schools. Otherwise, you may need to think seriously about whether you are willing to move if that is the only way you can get a teaching position you want. I found that the geographic location was an important consideration for me.

Next, keep in mind that you will be expected to research, write, and publish to some extent. You will want to have access to a good library and research materials, high-quality research assistants, and grants to support your research. You will also need a good support staff to assist with the typing and preparation of your writing. It is preferable to have a secretary who does not also work for ten other professors. Again this may sound obvious, but I was amazed at the differences among law school libraries and available support services.

Discuss with prospective employers what courses you would be teaching each semester. As you might guess, the subjects you want to teach and the courses you will be expected to teach may not be the same. If you feel strongly about what subjects you teach, make sure that the schools to which you are applying are aware of your preferences and that their curriculum needs are compatible with your desires. Another consideration is the amount of your course load. How many courses will you be expected to teach each semester? What is a typical course load for each faculty member, and are there provisions for release time for additional research?

Last, but probably most important, is the compatibility of the faculty. Too many law schools have faculties consisting of factions that do not get along with each other. Finding an environment in which you feel comfortable and in which you like most of, or at least a majority of, your colleagues can make teaching much more enjoyable. Having other faculty members who are supportive and available to give helpful advice is comforting. I have found that even if you have taught individual classes before, full-time teaching at a new law school can be stressful no matter how well-prepared you may think you are. Besides, one of the great joys of being a law school professor is the opportunity to share ideas—about both teaching and writing—with others whom you respect and from whom you can learn.

© 1982 by Sam Hurt

Why Be a Law Professor?

After going through this entire process, what is it like to be a law professor? And is it worth all the effort it takes to become one? To the last question, I can answer a resounding "yes."

My personal satisfaction as a law school professor is based in part upon my experiences as an attorney as well as the particular law school at which I have been fortunate to work. After taking the bar examination, I spent eleven years in practice, including time in private law firms and as a public defender. Although I learned a great deal in each job, many times I found myself frustrated that I did not have sufficient time to think about particular issues in depth. I did not have the luxury of focusing on problems that I chose to research because they were of specific interest to me. In other words, my time was usually devoted to thinking about and researching issues that were of interest to my clients. That, unfortunately, is the nature of most legal practice.

Law school teaching does give you the pleasure of choosing the issues about which you want to write and the opportunity to spend more time thinking about problems and creative solutions. Most law practices simply cannot invest the same amount of time or offer the same flexibility. In addition, academia offers professors the freedom to take whatever position on an issue they conclude is appropriate, without the constraints of advocating any particular client's viewpoint. I find that freedom to be refreshing. If you enjoy wrestling with intellectual issues, then this aspect of being a law professor should appeal to you.

Perhaps the most satisfying reward of being a professor is the gratification that comes from working with law students. This carries with it the knowledge that you may well have an impact upon your students' lives and futures as well as the quality of legal representation that their clients will receive. I have enjoyed teaching and have always found it to be a stimulating challenge. If engaging in dialogue with students is not a prospect that excites you, then perhaps you should reassess whether you truly want to teach.

Although as a law school professor you may miss the thrill of practice or of going to court, the trade-off is one that I have found to be well worthwhile. Besides, you still may have an opportunity to consult on actual cases if you have the time and the inclination.

In the final analysis, being a law professor is not totally idyllic. Teaching is hard work, and for each hour of class time, you will spend substantially more hours in preparation. Also, the research and writing portion of the job is often a solitary one. You need to be the sort of person who finds satisfaction from such individual effort. Finally, there can be a substantial difference between what you are likely to earn as a law professor and what you could earn in private practice.

You can probably tell by now that despite those caveats, being a law professor is one of the most challenging and interesting legal jobs available, and I recommend it highly.

I HAVE A DREAM
Minorities in the Profession

Grace E. Speights

Grace E. Speights talks straight from her personal experience about the reality minorities can expect in law school and in the profession. Contrasting myths with the "real world," she examines a range of issues, including confronting prejudice in law school, securing postgraduate employment, battling racism in practice, and learning the art of networking. With words of encouragement, author Speights challenges minority students to envision the struggles of those black leaders who made the road into the profession a lot easier.

In the eighteenth and nineteenth centuries, an apprenticeship was the primary vehicle to become a lawyer. Blacks desiring to become lawyers, however, faced a difficult challenge because most white lawyers would not sponsor blacks in an apprenticeship program. Macon B. Allen was able to find a sponsor, however, and in July of 1844, he became the first black lawyer in the United States.

By the end of the nineteenth century, law schools became the primary focus for legal training. Those law schools, however, were primarily white, and few blacks attended. Despite those odds, George Lewis Ruffin graduated from Harvard Law School in 1869, becoming the first black law school graduate in this nation.

Several decades later, Charles Hamilton Houston graduated from Harvard Law School in the top 5 percent of his class, having been the first black elected to the editorial board of the *Harvard Law Review*. He later went on to open one of the first black law firms in Washington, D.C.

If you are a minority student considering whether to attend law school, be mindful of the successful struggles of the Charles Hamilton

Grace E. Speights is a former judicial clerk to Chief Judge Aubrey E. Robinson Jr. of the United States District Court for the District of Columbia. She is currently a litigation associate in the Washington, D.C., office of Morgan, Lewis & Bockius.

Houstons, the George Lewis Ruffins, and the Macon B. Allens. Be aware of the myths concerning black lawyers, the reality of minorities in the profession, and the challenges that a minority group member faces upon entering law school.

The Myth

Many people may attempt to dissuade you from entering the legal profession. One of their primary reasons for discouraging you is the concern that there are too many lawyers, but this is a myth as it relates to minority lawyers. In 1987, there were approximately 672,000 lawyers in this country. Of that number, only 20,000 were black lawyers. In other words, in 1987 only 3 percent of this nation's lawyers were black. Similarly, in 1980 there were 26,700 judges in the state judiciaries. Only 469, or 1.8 percent, of those state judges were black.

Another myth surrounding minority lawyers relates to postgraduate employment. Many minority law students believe that their race is a positive factor in securing employment. This simply is not the case. Most employers do not go out of their way to seek minority applicants. They no longer have affirmative action programs or find it desirable, necessary, or attractive to hire minorities into their ranks. In fact, a substantial number of minority law students have difficulty in obtaining their first job after law school unless they are at the top of their class or on law review.

As you decide whether law school is the appropriate course for your career, it is important that you dispel the myths set forth above. Before entering law school, take a hard look at the realities of being a minority member in the profession.

The Reality

Minorities in the legal profession face several ongoing battles throughout their careers. First, there is the battle with racism, which is apparent in the hiring and promotion practices within the profession—resulting in minuscule numbers of black associates and partners within major firms and law departments of major corporations. In addition, minority law firms engage in the battle of racism on a daily basis in the neverending quest for clients and sources of power. Corporate clients, due to the badges of racism, are initially reluctant to hire minority law firms to represent them. Such firms are required to expend significant time and money to convince corporate clients that minority firms are just as qualified and competent as other law firms.

Second, minorities have an initial battle in attempting to enter law, which is a very close-knit profession, traditionally dominated by white males. This situation is akin to joining an elite country club or a fraternal organization. Cultural bias in admissions tests and the high costs of bar exams and bar dues also work to disadvantage minority lawyers.

Finally, minorities in the legal profession face the never-ending battle of survival within whatever type of organization they choose to practice. Since there are so few minorities in most of the practice organizations, a strong support system is often lacking. Sometimes this lack of support can lead to a serious loss of minorities within the ranks of the profession. Established groups such as the National Bar Association, its affiliates and divisions, the National Conference of Black Lawyers, and the National Association of Black Women Attorneys, however, can provide minorities within the profession with strong support and networking systems if minorities are committed to the existence and support of such organizations.

© 1985 by Sam Hurt

The Challenge

Given the realities minorities face in the profession, if you choose to go to law school you must be ready to meet the challenge. This challenge begins on the first day. Many of your professors and classmates may not believe that you are qualified to be in law school. They may initially question your ability and your competence. You may be urged to sit in the back of the classroom so that you will not be noticed. You *will* be noticed, unless you attend a predominantly black law school, because there will be few of you. You must be aggressive and confident in your abilities and commit yourself to learning the law well. Being prepared for class every day is a must, and you should go out of your way to voluntarily participate in classroom discussions. It is important that you overcome any reluc-

97

tance to visit your professors if you have a problem or need clarification on a topic.

If time and study habits permit, take part in extracurricular activities. Do not shy away from participation in law review, moot court competitions, or student government. In addition, join the student divisions of the National Bar Association, the American Bar Association, and other similar associations. These opportunities will enhance and sharpen your skills. They will put you on a par, or even better than that, with your classmates in terms of qualifications for postgraduate employment. In other words, you must make things happen. Make yourself unique, so that employers will find your background attractive.

The challenge is yours to meet. It won't be easy, but the obstacles are surmountable with hard work, persistence, drive, and determination. As you enter law school, envision the struggles of Macon B. Allen, George Lewis Ruffin, and Charles Hamilton Houston. Because of these gentlemen your road will be easier.

EVE, ESQ.
Women in Law

Lynn Hecht Schafran

Lynn Hecht Schafran confronts the remaining barriers for women and asks the question, "And why should men care?" Contrasting the historical with the current status of women in the law, she examines a broad range of issues, from combating employment barriers and securing employment with the right employer to finding a professional style. With a final thought, Schafran speaks of the unique and significant contributions women have made to the profession.

Why a special chapter on women in the profession, when women today constitute a third to a half of law school classes and occupy prestigious positions from a deanship of Columbia School of Law to a seat on the U.S. Supreme Court? The short answer is that despite the vast strides that women lawyers have made in recent years, despite the fact that women are practicing successfully and happily in every area of the profession, nowhere on the continuum from law school to the judiciary have women as a group attained full equal opportunity and professional acceptance.

Women entering the profession need to know what the remaining barriers are in order to recognize them as barriers and be prepared to deal with them. Men entering the profession should care equally about these barriers for several reasons.

Some barriers result from beliefs about the proper nature and role of women so deeply rooted in our culture that even men genuinely committed to equality perpetuate them unwittingly. The barriers labeled "women's issues" because they involve structuring work to accommodate family life and children are in fact issues for both sexes. The exclusion of

Lynn Hecht Schafran is an attorney and Director of the National Judicial Education Program to Promote Equality for Women and Men in the Courts, a project of the NOW Legal Defense and Education Fund in cooperation with the National Association of Women Judges. She is special counsel to the New York City Commission on the Status of Women and a member of the American Bar Association Commission on Women in the Profession.

"women's issues" and their viewpoints from law school and the profession has seriously compromised lawyers' abilities to represent their women clients.

Finally, it is a stock joke that law school teaches you to think like a lawyer: valuing rule-bound thinking over human experience and squeezing out all the passion and compassion. This way of teaching and practicing law is being questioned by students and scholars who find it antithetical to their personal morality and therefore a barrier to their participation in law school and the profession. There are men, too, who during law school and later in their professional careers as lawyers and judges have wondered where their values went. The exploration of this issue being spearheaded by feminist legal scholars should be of concern to everyone at every stage of professional life.

A Short History of Women in the Law

Understanding women's current status in the law requires some historical perspective. Women are not mentioned in the Constitution. Throughout most of the nineteenth century, women were legally classified with children and thus barred from such rights of full, adult citizenship as owning property, entering into contracts, and suing in their own names. Women could not vote until 1920. When the modern women's movement began in the early 1960s, women were still legally barred from many occupations and jury service, denied equal pay for equal work, denied equal fringe benefits, fired when they became pregnant, denied credit, and denied reproductive choice. Rape victims were cross-examined on every aspect of their sex lives, and convictions were rare. The terms "domestic violence" and "sexual harassment" had yet to be invented, much less made grounds for legal redress. It was not until 1971 that the U.S. Supreme Court used the Equal Protection Clause of the Fourteenth Amendment to strike down a sexually discriminatory statute. Women today still have no constitutional guarantee of equality under law.

Women's second-class status *under* the law was reflected in their status *in* the law. Law was the last profession to admit women in more than token numbers. It was not until the mid-1970s that the percentage of women in law school and practice reached double digits. Eighty percent of women practicing law in 1988 entered the profession after 1970.

Why was the law so resistant to women practitioners? Karen Berger Morello wrote in her history of women in the legal profession, *The Invisible Bar* (1987, pp. x–xi):

> The reasons for the resistance to women in the law can never be fully explained, but it is likely that it has to do with the

law's close relationship to power in our society. When Barbara J. Harris studied nineteenth century professional women in *Beyond Her Sphere,* comparing the difficulties women had in entering the legal and medical professions, she found that women faced greatest opposition from the bar. Harris and others who had examined the role of women in the legal system note that while entry into the medical profession might be justified as a natural extension of women's nurturing role, the law was clearly an all-male domain, closest to the center of power that was not to be invaded or changed by females.

The resistance to women in the profession was not a passive failure to welcome them with open arms, but an active effort to keep them out. In 1873, the U.S. Supreme Court denied a woman a license to practice law on the grounds that God and nature intended women for the domestic sphere and only men for the occupations of civil life. Law schools first refused to admit women (Harvard held out until 1950), then kept the number admitted artificially low by admitting a far smaller percentage of qualified women than men.

At law school, women were regularly accused of taking men's places just to get husbands and ignored in class except for the infamous "Ladies' Days," when only women students were called on, to discuss sexual assault cases or read poems. Female faculty role models were virtually nonexistent. In 1950 there were five women on tenure tracks at approved law schools. By 1960 the number had swelled to eleven. In 1970 65 percent of law schools had no women faculty members. In 1980 the national average for tenured female law faculty was 11 percent. Women never constituted more than 10 percent of law students until 1973. It took the need to fill law school seats during the Vietnam War and Title IX of the Education Amendments of 1972 barring sex discrimination in schools receiving federal funds to really open law schools to women.

Obtaining employment after law school was extraordinarily difficult, no matter how brilliant a woman's record. Many law firms and judges would not even interview women. After graduating among the top in her Stanford class in 1952, Supreme Court Justice Sandra Day O'Connor was offered a job as legal secretary by one of San Francisco's leading firms. When D.C. Circuit Court of Appeals Judge Ruth Bader Ginsburg graduated first in her class from Columbia in 1959, she could not obtain a clerkship with the Second Circuit Court of Appeals in New York. The few firms that actually hired women in the fifties and sixties expected them to do trusts and estates work and stay in the library. Women did not go to court and had no client contact. Most women lawyers turned to government service, but only on the civil side. Federal and state prosecutors made it clear that they would have no women on their teams. The only area of criminal law open to women was legal services for the indigent, where the pay was (and is) very low. The few women in private practice had to content themselves with the one area of the law thought to be appropriate for them: matrimonials and juveniles—the "domestic sphere" of the law.

The organized bar, too, organized to keep women out. The American Bar Association, for example, refused to admit women until 1935. Even after admitting women to membership and profiting from their dues, many bar associations denied women any visible participation on committees or as officers.

The judiciary, that most obvious seat and symbol of power, was totally off-limits. Although Iowa in 1869 was the first state to admit a woman to practice, it was another 114 years before Iowa had a woman judge. By 1987, women constituted still less than 8 percent of federal and state judges. Although one woman had been appointed to the U.S. Supreme Court in 1981, twenty-one states had never had a woman on their highest court.

Women made up only 4 percent of the legal profession in 1970 (11,000) and still only 17 percent in 1986 (47,920). An American Bar Association survey revealed that as late as 1983, 65 percent of male attorneys had no female colleagues. The fact that the vast majority of today's attorneys and judges are white men who went through law school and most of their professional lives with no women peers and no opportunity to relate to women as working friends puts into context the perspective of these men and their attitudes toward the women now beginning to become a presence in the legal profession.

Women in the Legal Profession Today

As the percentage of women lawyers began to increase in the mid-1970s, questions were raised about whether the law would change women or women would change the law. There is no question that women lawyers changed the law, in the sense of reforming sex discrimination statutes, utilizing remedial statutes for women clients' benefit, and bringing to national attention the issue of gender bias in the courts as it affects both litigants and lawyers. Studies ranging from Cynthia Epstein's comprehensive book *Women in the Law* (1981), exploring the problems of women trying to integrate this all-male profession during the 1970s, to a study released by the Boston Bar Association in January 1988 revealed that despite significant advances for women in a relatively short time, and whether women attempt to succeed by conforming to the male role model or creating their own, barriers remain to women's full integration into the profession.

The Law School Experience

Women today are a critical mass in law schools, and Ladies' Days are a thing of the past, but in 1985 the Harvard Law Women's Association found it necessary to provide the faculty with a pamphlet about how to conduct a nonsexist, nonracist classroom, including the instruction "Don't Tell Sexist Jokes, Stories, Poems or Parables." One contracts professor begins each year by asking women students whether any of them are feminists, as if feminism were something despicable rather than a commitment to sexual equality. Betsy Levin, executive director of the Association of American Law Schools, reported to the ABA Commission on the Profession in 1988 that during her 1981–87 term as dean of the University of Colorado School of Law, she saw an increase in sexist slurs written on campus posters and challenges to women teachers' authority.

On a deeper level, in 1987 three Yale Law professors undertook a formal study of why many women find the law school experience so dissatisfying. The study was prompted by issues raised by a group of first-year women students in 1985. As Professor Lucinda M. Finley, one of the investigators, described it in the preliminary report:

> Their presentation went well beyond the usual gamut of law student gripes, but instead drew on their experiences as women in a traditionally male-dominated environment to point out ways that the structure and values of legal education alienated them and discouraged the development of many of the perspectives and skills that they thought important to cultivate as lawyers and human beings.

These students reported feeling frustrated and silenced by what they perceived as male faculty members' and students' overinvolvement with abstractions and rules, lack of attention to the human and social context

103

of cases, and dismissal of observations that women students made based on their life experiences. These students also cited concerns that have been cited in studies of educational institutions at every level. For example, a woman's answer to a teacher's question draws little response, but when a man makes the same point a few moments later, the teacher takes it up with interest.

What is taught in law school is as much a problem as the way it is taught. Recently, a number of women law professors examined casebooks, particularly those in criminal law. Their study revealed that in the seven most widely used criminal law casebooks, domestic violence is barely discussed and rape is presented as an exercise in the manufacture of defenses. The 1985 edition of one of the most widely used criminal law casebooks omits rape altogether. Although family law cases dealing with divorce, alimony, child support, and the enforcement of support awards are the leading category of cases on almost every state's civil docket and a major factor in the growing impoverishment of women and the children in their custody, some schools do not even offer a class in family law.

Another problem is that women law faculty members are still few and unevenly distributed. At the schools with a substantial number of women faculty members, such as Brooklyn Law School, it appears that women students are active participants in class and feel well integrated into the school. Where women faculty members are oddities, women students, too, feel like outsiders.

These issues of women students' dissatisfaction, the failure to include women's perspectives and concerns in casebooks and class discussions, and the recruitment of more women faculty members are gaining increased attention. By the time you reach law school, they may be to some extent ameliorated. But they will not have vanished, and you should be prepared to deal with them. Involving yourself in or creating an organization focused on the entire spectrum of "women's issues"—an organization that should include men—is one way to seek change from an institutional base rather than go it alone.

Although to date those who have written about their disenchantment with law school's abstraction and devaluation of individual experience have been women, this is an issue for men as well. There is much debate in social science, moral philosophy, and other circles about whether women tend to value caring and connectedness significantly more than men do. But it is clear that there are men in the profession whose value systems reflect those same concerns. Supreme Court Justice William Brennan, in a 1987 speech to the Association of the Bar of the City of New York entitled "Reason, Passion and the 'Progress of the Law,'" decried the formalist concept of law that supposed there was a mechanical rule for everything just waiting to be discovered. "An appreciation for the dialogue between head and heart is precisely what was missing from the formalist conception of judging. . . . In the bureaucratic welfare state of the late twentieth century what we need most acutely is the passion that understands the pulse of life beneath the official version of events." (The Record, Association of the Bar of the City of New York, December 1987, 42:947.)

Men should support serious discussion of "women's issues" in law school classes in order to learn not only how the law is distorted by gender stereotypes, but how these stereotypes constrain the lives of men as well as women. Most important, failure to address these issues undermines both sexes' professional competence. Gender bias in all its forms—stereotypes about the nature and role of women and men, society's perception of the value of women and men and so-called "women's work," and myths and misconceptions about the social and economic realities of women's and men's lives—is pervasive in the application, interpretation, and enforcement of the law and often the law itself.

These issues affect men and women alike. You are not competent to prosecute a rape case if you know nothing of how the law's and society's image of women as temptresses who consent and then cry rape can prejudice judge and jury. You are not competent to defend a woman who kills her violently abusive husband if you know nothing of the battered woman syndrome. You are not competent to represent a woman in certain medical malpractice cases if you know nothing of the medical profession's history of telling women that their pains are all in their head and prescribing tranquilizers for serious physical problems. You are not competent to secure an equitable divorce settlement for a 50-year-old lifetime homemaker if you know nothing of how society devalues the economic worth of homemaker work and the extreme difficulty women have in obtaining paid employment above minimum wage.

What to Look For in an Employer

Deciding where to work at any point in your career should include consideration of whether the employer considers women and families. Depending on the type of employer, does the firm have women partners, does the prosecutor's office have women bureau chiefs, does the government agency have women in policymaking positions—and are women in these positions in more than token numbers? Does the employer have a written, comprehensive sexual harassment policy with meaningful enforcement provisions?

As more women enter the work force, increasing attention is being given to maternity policies. Some legal employers are highly responsive to these needs. Others are totally resistant. Although the legal profession has always coped with men taking leaves to run for office, to fulfill military reserve obligations, or for other nonfamily purposes, taking time out for children has been treated as indicating lack of seriousness and dedication to the profession. These attitudes are slowly beginning to change. Some legal employers in both the private and public sectors have seen that offering good family policies is actually a recruitment tool for them because it enables them to attract and retain top women. Many women have found their career with a given employer wrecked because they were forced into ad hoc negotiations and refused any accommodation.

Look for a written family leave policy that allows time off for mothers and fathers for childbirth, adoption, children's illness, and the needs of dependent relatives. (Women are usually the care givers not only for their children, but for their own, and often their husband's, parents.) Look for a written policy with respect to part-time work, flextime and job sharing, and salary proration under these options, and learn how working an alternative schedule affects decisions about partnership and promotion. Find out whether lawyers who actually availed themselves of these policies advanced with their peers or were penalized.

Job Interviews

Job interviews can be unpleasant because, despite the Equal Employment Opportunity Commission's guidelines about what employers may ask consistent with antidiscrimination laws, some judges and lawyers continue to ask women questions about whether they are married, their children and plans for children, and whether they have their husbands' permission to seek employment. Remarks such as, "You're so pretty; I don't care about your grades" and requests for dates are also not uncommon. Telling the interviewer off is fine if you don't want the job, but it is not diplomatic if you do. Law school interviews offer a small measure of protection. Encourage your placement office to advise interviewers that biased questioning is not permitted and will not be ignored. Report such questioning to the placement office. Law schools have taken a variety of actions in these situations, from admonitory letters to barring the firm from on-campus recruiting for a year.

Asking about family leave and part-time work policies during interviews can be tricky. Because some employers already assume that women's priorities place family a distinct first ahead of work and worry that the money, time, and effort invested in training women will be wasted because they will just have babies and stay home or leave town when their husbands are transferred, asking about relevant policies at your interview simply confirms the belief that women are not adequately committed to the profession. You can have some control over this problem when you are interviewing while still at law school by encouraging your placement office to require campus interviewers to complete a data sheet that will give you the critical information for which you may hesitate to ask.

Subsequent to law school you can contact your law school placement office to obtain current information on these points. If the school does not have it, you will have to ask for this information if the employer does not offer it orally or in written form. Family leave and sexual harassment policies are too important to be left to on-the-job surprises. Assume that any interviewer whose nose is put out of joint by your asking about these policies is not someone with whom you would want to work.

Employment Barriers

To varying degrees, women continue to find barriers to full equal employment opportunity throughout the legal profession. Criminal justice has been the most difficult field for women to crack because of its image as a macho preserve. Only one woman has ever been elected attorney general of her state. Women U.S. attorneys are almost as rare. Many men prosecutors fear that women will spoil the camaraderie of the office or won't be able to get along with the police. There are extremely few women doing white-collar criminal defense work.

A *National Law Journal* study of the country's 250 largest law firms revealed that although as of September 30, 1987, 40 percent of the associates hired in the prior two years were women, women constitute only 23 percent of the lawyers at these firms and less than 8 percent of the partners (1,546 women out of 19,610 partners). At the current rate of increase, by the year 2000 only one in five partners will be women. The *National Law Journal* noted that a 1985 forecast that the percentage rate of women partners would have doubled or trebled by 1988 or 1989 had "fizzled, in part, because more and more female attorneys, particularly on the associate level, are showing dissatisfaction with life at the megafirms and are leaving for smaller firms, part-time work, teaching or other alternatives." Even women who become partners in large firms sometimes find that they are not welcomed into the management structure of their firms.

Client resistance to women attorneys continues to be a problem in both law firms and corporate legal departments. A client who brings business to a firm or a manager who brings a problem to the legal department may say flatly that he does not want a woman on the case. Many law firms and general counsels (the chief "in-house" lawyers for a company or institution) insist that the client take the lawyer assigned, regardless of sex. But there are reports from corporate counsel that insisting sometimes leads to the manager's cutting back on consultation with the legal department and finding ways to give work to outside counsel who accept their sexist dictates.

Small firms, particularly in more rural areas, sometimes do not want to hire women at all or let them try only family law cases. Women are still a small percentage of law school faculty members—at some schools there is only one woman teaching—and those who raise feminist issues may be denigrated by their colleagues and students and denied tenure.

Women seeking judgeships continue to be asked questions about their husbands and children by judicial selection commissions. Even women on the bench find that some male colleagues have difficulty in accepting them. Moreover, under the Reagan Administration the appointment rate for women to the federal bench was half what it was under the Carter Administration (8.6 percent compared to 15 percent), which means that in this critical area women are actually moving backward.

Compensation

Several bar association studies have shown a sharp disparity between men and women attorneys' earnings. A 1987 ABA study, for example, showed men's median earnings at $71,710 and women's at $40,190. According to the researchers, this disparity cannot be wholly explained by the fact that women as a group are younger than men, have fewer years in practice, and work in lower-paying government and public-sector jobs than do men.

Sexual Harassment

Sexual harassment—demanding sexual favors in exchange for grades, hiring, promotion, or retention and verbal or physical conduct of a sexual nature that creates an offensive work environment—is as prevalent in law schools and the legal profession as it is in every other academic and business setting. While the landmark 1984 case that held that employment discrimination laws do apply to partnerships was pending before the U.S. Supreme Court, the defending law firm subjected its women summer associates to an impromptu bathing suit contest during the firm's summer outing. Some women said they did not mind, but others were appalled. None was willing to object, however, lest she be branded a bad sport and not offered a permanent position. A midwestern law school that regularly places students as law clerks in firms in its city was advised that one partner at a particular firm was engaging in extreme verbal sexual harassment. The placement office's only response was that it would stop placing women with that firm.

Judges have been disciplined and removed from the bench for sexually harassing women attorneys and court employees. Some young women associates have had their careers derailed at their firms by the following scenario. An older male partner and a young female associate are out of town on a case. Late at night, after a few drinks, he knocks on her door. Whether she says yes or no, the next morning he is mortified and wants to distance himself from her and any memory of the event. The next time she is assigned to his team he says he doesn't want her, her work the last time just wasn't up to snuff, and so begins the insidious destruction of her professional reputation in the firm. Some women who have lived through this experience suggest trying to defuse it at the start by treating it lightly, saying, "No, it's late, let's both forget this happened and go on doing good work together." But there are no easy answers.

A written, comprehensive sexual harassment policy with teeth for schools and employers is necessary. This ensures that the harassing supervisor, interviewer, or coworker can be reported.

Finding a Professional Style

Sociologists use the term "double bind" to describe the dilemma facing all professional women in establishing a behavioral style that is both professionally effective and personally comfortable. The woman who displays stereotypically feminine traits such as passivity, dependence, deference, soft-spokenness, and emotionalism is perceived as too soft to do the job. The woman who displays the so-called "competency cluster" of traits associated with men—aggressiveness, independence, ambition, rationality, action—is put down as pushy and abrasive. This is a major problem for women attorneys throughout the country.

In *Trial* magazine, Barbara Billauer, a litigation partner in a large New York firm, recently discussed the consequences of the double bind for women litigators ("The Frustrations of Women Lawyers," July 1987, p. 7).

> . . . there is a dichotomy between societal perception of "appropriate" female behavior and necessary "lawyer-like" behavior. Until this dichotomy is resolved, many women will continue to experience job dissatisfaction and frustration. . . .

> The ABA Standards Relating to the Prosecution and Defense Function state

> > Advocacy is not for the timid, the meek or the retiring. Our system of justice is inherently contentious in nature, albeit bounded by the rules of professional ethics and decorum, and it demands the lawyer have the urge for the vigorous contest.

To succeed as a lawyer, in other words, one needs skills not perceived as feminine, and often not tolerated in a woman. . . . The woman lawyer who has mastered such skills and learned how to use them effectively on behalf of clients is often confronted with derogatory remarks and sometimes even open hostility by an adversary she has beaten. In fact, many men cannot handle being beaten by a woman in the courtroom, which has traditionally been regarded as the last bastion of male supremacy in the law.

This problem of expectation about style has ramifications beyond the courtroom. Men litigators sometimes complain that whereas men they oppose at trial can afterward forget the fight and be friendly, women adversaries hold a grudge and are standoffish. Although this is undoubtedly true in some cases, what is actually happening is that men's criteria for "friendliness" from a woman are based on stereotyped notions of how women should behave in social/romantic relationships rather than on professional norms. Thus, the woman adversary who is matter-of-fact rather than admiring after a trial is put down as having a chip on her shoulder.

Another aspect of the style problem is that men sometimes give even highly successful women lawyers criticism and negative performance evaluation because the women use different styles, skills, and strategies. We have not yet reached the point at which women are judged by how effective they are rather than whether their approaches to work are similar to those of men.

© 1986 by Sam Hurt

Women Lawyers in Court

Some judges, lawyers, and court personnel have difficulty in accepting women as professionals. This is reflected in their behavior toward women lawyers and judicial clerks that includes overly familiar forms of address ("Susie" or "young lady" instead of "Ms." or "Counselor"), comments on personal appearance that are sometimes well-meant but often made at inappropriate times (how does a lawyer establish her credibility with the jury when the judge's compliment has just defined her as a fashion plate?), remarks that demean women and sexist "jokes," and verbal and sometimes physical advances. Studies in several states throughout the 1980s showed that these behaviors occur with frequency and that male attorneys engage in them even more than judges and court personnel.

When women attorneys object to these behaviors, they are often told that this is trivial, that they are making a mountain out of a molehill, or that anything is fair as a litigation tactic. But these behaviors are more than personally insulting. They undermine the credibility of the attorney as a professional and, by extension, that of her client. They force the attorney to think about whether it advantages or disadvantages her client's case to respond rather than think about the case itself. And as to litigation tactics, we do not permit race-baiting in the courts, so why do we permit this?

In 1980, the National Judicial Education Program to Promote Equality for Women and Men in the Courts, a project of the NOW Legal Defense and Education Fund in cooperation with the National Association of Women Judges, began to present seminars at judges' and lawyers' continuing education programs to make them aware of how gender bias affects decision making and the courtroom interaction. These educational programs led to a series of task forces, which were established by the chief justices of approximately twenty states mandated to investigate the nature and extent of gender bias in their own state court systems and recommend ways to eliminate it. Although there is evidence that gender bias in court interaction is abating as a consequence of this kind of investigation and education, this is another of the barriers still facing women in the profession about which it is important to be forewarned.

A final point relating to women in the courts is women's unequal access to important fee-generating appointments. In many states, judges appoint lawyers to control property or represent clients in a wide variety of civil and criminal cases. Women lawyers across the country report that few judges appoint women to receiverships, condemnations, and other kinds of business cases that pay well. On the civil side, women are usually appointed as guardians *ad litem* to represent children in family disputes, once again the "domestic sphere" of the law. In criminal cases, women are appointed to represent women accused of misdemeanors, while men are appointed to represent men in the kinds of felony cases that give a lawyer important experience and community visibility.

Rainmaking

"Rainmaking," more politely termed "client development," means bringing in business. Always an element in consideration for law firm

111

partnership, rainmaking has grown in importance in recent years as law firm economics have forced firms into open competition for clients. Rainmaking has long been more difficult for women than men for several reasons. Men's college and law school roommates and luncheon and golf club friends are themselves in various businesses and professions and have legal business to give out. Women could not, and in many places still cannot, join the luncheon and golf clubs where men have long made and maintained their business contacts.

Men with reason to hire attorneys are often uncomfortable hiring a woman unless they know her well or she has an essential expertise. The threshold problem, which may take years to overcome, is that some segments of our society still assume that a man is competent until proven otherwise, and a woman is less than competent until proven otherwise. This presents a Catch-22 for the woman lawyer who would be a rainmaker. She cannot establish business contacts because she is presumed incompetent, and she cannot prove herself competent until she gets the business. This barrier should diminish as more women open businesses and become general counsels and are in a position to place business with women friends.

If you aspire to law firm partnership, take every opportunity to learn about rainmaking (bar associations, for example, often offer seminars on client development), because it is an area on which you will be judged. Although law firms are generally convinced of the ability of their women lawyers to do the work, they are wary of women's ability to bring in the work.

Conclusion

Despite their small number, women lawyers have already made a unique and significant contribution to the profession. The barriers to women's full integration into the profession described in this chapter will diminish as the number of women lawyers and judges increases, but numbers are not enough, and women cannot do it alone. Only when lawyers of both sexes throughout the profession understand what these barriers are, how they affect the professional and personal lives of women and men, and how they are reflected in inadequate client representation and gender-biased judging can the profession begin to grapple meaningfully with these problems. Only a conscious, consistent, and ongoing effort that begins in law schools and is carried through in every aspect of the profession can eliminate them.

MAKING THE DECISION FOR LAW

WHEEL OF FORTUNE
Choosing the Right Law School

Mark P. Cardinalli and Paul D. Hoskins

Choosing a law school can be an arduous and confusing task. Mark P. Cardinalli and Paul D. Hoskins provide some guidelines to bring order to the confusion and suggest a practical approach to choosing a school that is a good fit for you.

Choosing a law school may well be the most important professional decision a law student makes. It should not be made based on casual information or your acquaintance with alumni who enjoyed attending a particular school. Unfortunately, there are no magic formulas into which a prospective law student's preferences may be plugged to identify the ideal law school for that student.

Law schools come in all shapes and sizes and can be found in most states in a variety of environments. Each school is unique in its combination of location, programs, facilities, and approach to the study of law. Research facilities and extracurricular opportunities vary widely from institution to institution, as do admissions requirements and tuition rates.

You need to learn as much as possible about a prospective school and make an honest self-appraisal of your personal, professional, and financial circumstances and goals. This chapter suggests various factors by which law schools can be differentiated and suggests a practical approach to arriving at a list of schools that might be right for you.

Factors to Consider

The first step is to make an honest evaluation of your chances of being admitted to a given school. Being a shoo-in for admission is not neces-

---

Mark P. Cardinalli practices litigation with David Allen & Associates in Reno, Nevada. He graduated from the University of the Pacific McGeorge School of Law in Sacramento. Paul D. Hoskins is a civil litigator in Sacramento. He is also a McGeorge alumnus who graduated in 1985.

sary, but you should limit your applications to schools likely to admit you. Most schools charge a nonrefundable application fee, so it becomes expensive to apply to a lot of schools for which your qualifications are clearly inadequate.

The most important criteria for admission to law school are your undergraduate grade point average and Law School Admission Test score. The *Prelaw Handbook,* generally available in university bookstores, provides a chart for most of the ABA-approved law schools showing LSAT score and GPA ranges for the previous year's applicants and admittees. Some schools will also provide this data directly to students upon request.

There is a caveat to all of this: most schools do not rely exclusively on these two criteria in determining admissions eligibility, so do not despair if your numbers do not meet your dream school's expectations. Many schools also consider life experiences and extracurricular activities, as well as factors such as geographic location and minority status.

If your credentials are insufficient for you to gain admission to one of the 175 ABA-accredited law schools, you may want to consider a non-ABA-accredited, state-approved school. Few states permit graduates of unaccredited schools to sit for the bar exam. Check the requirements of those states in which you might be interested in practicing before you choose an unaccredited school.

As you evaluate those schools to which you might be admitted, you need to investigate and consider the schools' reputation, programs, and location. Approximately twenty schools are known as "national" rather than "state" schools. National law schools generally have a broad reputation outside the state in which they are located and do not emphasize the law of that particular state. A nationally known school offers greater access to a national network of job opportunities and is more apt to have law firms and corporations from across the nation participating in its on-campus interview process. A smaller or lesser-known school is more apt to attract only local or statewide firms or perhaps not even have on-campus interview opportunities.

Many state law schools, on the other hand, are geared toward preparing their students for that state's bar exam, although other state schools consider their main responsibility to be to teach the law and let each student worry about passing the bar. Often, state law schools have a higher bar passage rate than better-known national law schools. If you have not done well on standardized tests in the past or just lack confidence in your ability to pass the bar, going to a school with a high pass rate is a very practical consideration.

If you are interested in a specific area of law, you may want to choose a school with a strong program in that area. Those interested in litigation often choose schools with hands-on legal clinics in which students, under the supervision and guidance of professors and practicing attorneys, assist clients in resolving legal disputes. Similarly, if you're interested in an area such as international, environmental, or communications law, you will want to attend a school with a variety of courses in that area taught by recognized professors. Students considering a joint-degree program with another school at the university (such as the business school) should consider the caliber of the other school and the quality of the overall joint program.

The students, your day-to-day colleagues for three years, are another part of the law school package. Although most law schools have a demographically diverse group of students, some schools have a special emphasis, such as church-affiliated schools or schools with predominantly minority students.

Geography enters the law school decision in two ways—where you want to be for three years and where you want to be afterward. Family or other personal considerations may dictate going to school in a particular state or area of the country. Where you wish to practice after graduation should also be considered. Nationally known schools offer better employment opportunities, but if you know you want to work and live in a particular area, going to school there can be an advantage. Generally, there will be a lot of alumni working in the area, especially if the school is a small one. All things being equal, and sometimes even when they are not, a law firm may hire a student from a school that is already represented in the firm over another one who graduated from an unknown school.

Each law school has its own personality, and you will want to choose one that is compatible with your own. Some schools admit only a select few and expect every one of them to graduate three years later. Others admit more marginal students and allow a natural attrition rate to determine the size of the graduating class. Some schools encourage competition among their students, while others treat each student individually.

117

A visit to the school during the semester is usually the best way to get a feel for the atmosphere. Be aware that at every law school the atmosphere is inordinately more tense as exam period approaches, so don't judge a school too harshly by its December mood. While you're there, you can also check out the physical facilities and determine whether you want to spend three years in those particular hallowed halls.

Finally, to the vast majority of prospective law students who are not independently wealthy, financial considerations are important in selecting a law school. There is enough pressure in going to law school without having to worry about where the money for the next day's meals or next term's tuition is coming from.

Tuition, fees, and book expenses are but a small part of the overall cost of going to law school. Students are also required to pay for bar exams, bar review courses, resume services, study aids, and school supplies during the course of three years in law school. The cost of living in the area in which the school is located can also dramatically affect the total law school bill.

Most schools discourage students from having a job during their first year of study, and most students find that they are able to work only part-time during the final two years. If term-time work is necessary, as it is for a vast majority of students, learn the nature of the local job market, and find out whether the school has a placement office that can assist in locating suitable part-time employment.

There is a ray of sunshine through this financial cloud. Financial aid is available in all ABA-accredited schools, as well as at some nonaccredited schools. Federally subsidized loan programs are also available at most schools. These loans require either no payments until after graduation or payment of only interest until the student graduates. Finally, most of the individual schools have other grants and scholarships available. While academic performance remains an important criterion for many of these grants, others are based solely on financial need or consider student activities and employment experience.

If the cost of law school still appears staggering or if you are not prepared for three more years on a student budget, you may want to consider attending law school at night. Night programs require four years of study instead of three. Working full-time, attending class four nights a week, and studying while maintaining your sanity is a grueling endeavor. However, you may find that your personal circumstances mesh more effectively with an evening program than with a full-time one.

A Practical Approach

Once you have made this honest self-evaluation, you still must choose a law school. Even after exhaustive analysis, more than one school will be likely to fit all of your personal, professional, and financial needs. Here is a practical approach to narrow the number of schools to which you apply.

You are well-advised not to put all your application eggs in one basket. Unless you have very good friends in very high places (or have compromising pictures of the dean of admissions), there is no guarantee that you will be accepted by any particular law school. Applying to several schools where admissions criteria match your credentials will increase your chances of acceptance into at least one school.

Make a list that ultimately will be pared to those schools to which you will send applications. The first group of schools on your list should be all of those that you have always wanted to attend. This group probably will not include very many schools and could have as few as zero. It could also include all those schools to which your parents and friends have insisted you apply.

The second group of schools should be those to which you believe you have a good chance of being admitted based solely on your GPA and LSAT numbers. The schools in this group that remain on the list after final paring will be your fallbacks in case the schools on your "want" list all reject you.

The third group on the list should contain the names of those schools that consider factors, other than the GPA and LSAT numbers, that are applicable to you. These can include any significant work history or extracurricular activities, as well as your minority status, heritage, and religious affiliation.

The fourth group of schools on the list should be those that have the special programs and honors that correspond to your professional goals. This list should include those schools that offer any Master of Laws programs that might interest you.

The final group of schools on the list should contain those located in the area where you would prefer to go to school and/or practice law. If this area is an entire state and the state has a large number of law schools (such as California and New York), you should try to narrow your preference to a certain area or areas within the state.

The list should now consist of five groups containing the names of all those schools that you might attend—those that you want to attend, those that will probably accept you, those that might accept you, and those that fit your personal and professional needs—and it can now be pared down to a workable number, depending on your application budget. If the total amount of application fees for the schools on your list does not exceed your application budget, there is no reason why you should not apply to all of them.

If, as will generally be the case, this list contains more schools than you can afford to apply to, begin to narrow it down. Look at the list as a whole and note the schools that appear in every category. These are your first-choice schools for application.

Whatever the process you use to further reduce the list, be careful to apply to enough schools to maximize your chances of acceptance. After being accepted by as many schools as possible, you can then use the information gleaned from your self-evaluation to reject those schools that do not meet your personal needs, professional goals, and financial considerations.

A final word: law school can be hard, fun, exciting, depressing, rewarding, tense, competitive, disappointing, boring, and a drain on normal personal activities and relationships. You will be doing a disservice to yourself and those around you who care about you if you pick a law school randomly or based solely on the advice of friends, relatives, or alumni. By evaluating your own needs and goals prior to attending school, you will maximize both the education you receive and your enjoyment of the legal education process.

CAN ANYBODY PLAY?
The Law School
Admissions Game

Michael D. Rappaport

Where better to go for advice on getting into law school than to someone who is responsible for the evaluation of thousands of admissions applications a year? In this chapter, UCLA Dean of Admissions Michael D. Rappaport answers some of the questions you may have about the law school applications process. He counsels that getting into law school might not be as difficult as you think.

Getting into law school isn't easy, but it might not be as hard as you think. In my capacity as the Dean of Admissions at the UCLA School of Law, I am often asked how an applicant can improve the likelihood of earning admission. Having a strong undergraduate background helps, but getting the right information about where to apply to law school and how to apply is also important. This chapter answers the questions most frequently asked about preparing for and getting accepted into law school.

When Should You Start to Prepare for Law School?

Deciding on a legal career as a preteen is not necessary, and many successful law students never considered a legal career until after graduating from college. However, some people begin their preparation for law school in the earliest stages of their undergraduate college career. This kind of early preparation can include selecting classes that will be helpful later in law school in general or in a particular substantive area of the

---

Michael D. Rappaport, currently Dean of Admissions for the UCLA School of Law, has been working with the admissions process since 1970. He frequently lectures and advises on the subject of law school admissions and is also engaged in the practice of labor arbitration.

law in which you would like to specialize, maintaining a good grade point average, and even choosing which undergraduate university to attend.

In one way or another, admissions committees take into account the reputation of an applicant's undergraduate school. Some law schools have developed computerized models that measure the competition at undergraduate schools and use that as a factor in adjusting an applicant's undergraduate grade point average.

Is It Important to Pursue a Particular Major in Undergraduate School?

The traditional perception that you should major in political science or history if you want to go to law school is misleading. The skills, rather than the major, are the important thing. Writing, analytical, and oral communication skills are important to success in law school.

As an undergraduate, you should go out of your way to seek courses that demand papers and writing exercises. Courses in science, math, philosophy, and logic will encourage the development of analytical skills. Courses or activities such as debate and rhetoric develop speaking skills.

What Weight Will Be Given to Undergraduate Extracurricular Activities?

A solid academic record and a good LSAT score open the door to law school. Extracurricular activities are generally endorsed by law school admissions officers, but they are unlikely to be among the most important factors in the admissions decision.

Where Can You Get Information About Law Schools Before Deciding Where to Apply?

The *Prelaw Handbook*, published by the Law School Admission Council, the American Bar Association, and the Association of American Law Schools, contains a description of virtually every major law school in the United States. Its profiles include the average LSAT score and average undergraduate GPA for admission and indicate your own chances of admission at a particular school.

Another often-overlooked resource is the prelaw adviser. Granted, prelaw advisers at some schools may be junior members of the faculty having no particular experience with law school, but many of them are dedicated professionals who can provide valuable assistance. Some universities also have prelaw clubs that sponsor programs featuring speakers familiar with the law school admissions process.

You can also request information directly from the law schools. Many schools publish informational booklets for distribution at no cost. Some law schools sponsor an orientation day that you can attend, or they participate in prelaw day forums at area undergraduate schools.

What Is the LSAT?

Contrary to popular belief, the LSAT is not a devious means of frustrating and eliminating potential law school applicants. Nor is it a warm-up for the bar exam—the bar exam is much, much worse. The LSAT, formally known as the Law School Admission Test, is a prerequisite to admission to law school. The score for the 4-hour examination is reported as part of the application process. Security procedures are followed strictly to ensure that the person for whom the test score will be reported actually sits for the examination.

The LSAT tests reading comprehension, logical reasoning, and facts and issues analysis in much the same way as do undergraduate admissions tests. It also may include presentation of a fact situation to be solved by essay answer, as a writing exercise.

The LSAT is designed to predict only success in the first year of law school. Like it or not, most statistical information available tends to suggest that the LSAT *is* an excellent predictor, and law schools tend to rely quite heavily on the scores when selecting applicants for admission. Obviously, some law schools will have higher score requirements than others.

How Should You Prepare to Take the LSAT?

In theory, the LSAT measures analytical skills and reading and writing skills that take years to develop; nevertheless, it is very important to prepare for the LSAT by familiarizing yourself with how the exam tests that knowledge. Over the last ten years or so, an entire industry has grown up around the LSAT by providing test preparation courses. These courses take a wide variety of forms, and some of the private courses can be quite expensive. There is a common perception that taking such a course is essential to earning a competitive score on the test. Taking a commercial prep course is *not* necessary to successfully taking the exam. That is not to say that preparation courses are not very helpful, only that there are alternatives.

Potential applicants are furnished with instructions and with sample LSAT questions when they register. Commercial publications provide more extensive, but similar, information. Many undergraduate schools and college extension programs also offer LSAT preparation courses. However you choose to familiarize yourself with the exam, the important thing is that you do.

When Should You Take the LSAT?

Law school advisers urge applicants to take the test no later than the fall prior to the year in which they plan to apply. While some law schools accept results from the December test, waiting may place an applicant at a distinct disadvantage by eliminating the opportunity to retake the test if necessary. Waiting until the last possible test time also can be risky since you could wake up on the morning of the test with the flu or with a car that won't start.

Taking an early test gives you the opportunity to receive your score before deciding where to apply, so that you can more realistically assess your ability of meeting the admissions standards of the law schools you consider. You may be able to retake the test in hope of achieving a higher score. Many schools accept the scores from a second test, but they may average the scores from both tests for consideration in the admissions process.

Is There a Trick to the Application Procedure?

Law school application forms often surprise people with their brevity. Nonetheless, particular questions are asked for a reason. Answering the questions asked as carefully, concisely, and accurately as possible is always in an applicant's best interest.

Most law schools ask the applicant to submit a personal statement in essay form as part of the application process. Frequently, the personal statement is used as a device to determine which applicants within a group of similar applicants with similar academic records should be admitted.

Take the time to read and consider the question being asked and to answer it specifically. Although there is little likelihood that a school would turn down otherwise desirable applicants because they did not answer the specific question asked, borderline applicants must use the opportunity to make a personal statement to their best advantage.

If an applicant has a particularly difficult major, has been in an honors program, or has taken courses in a department in which grades are significantly lower than in other departments, it should be brought out in the personal statement. The personal statement is an opportunity to explain personal academic weaknesses as well as strengths, for example, that particularly difficult courses one year or personal problems that interfered with studies are responsible for low grades.

Finally, care and neatness count. In a sense, the personal statement is the first and perhaps the most important "brief" that you will write. If you don't take the time to do it properly, an admissions committee is not likely to give it a great deal of consideration either.

WINGTIPS by Michael Goodman

How Important Are Letters of Recommendation?

Although some law schools value letters from faculty members, friends of the family, alumni, politicians, judges, etc., for the most part these letters are not regarded as particularly useful. If a law school receives 4,000 applications and the average applicant sends in three letters of recommendation, the admissions committee can look forward to receiving over 12,000 letters of recommendation, which must be opened, sorted, filed, and eventually read.

The typical letter states simply, "So and So was a student in my class. He/she is very bright and articulate. I'm sure he/she will make a fine attorney. I have no hesitation in recommending him/her to your law school. Yours truly, Professor Thus and Such." A letter like this is not of much value in distinguishing one applicant from the rest. By far the best letter is one that goes something like, "So and So was a student in my class. I have been teaching at this institution for twenty-five years, and I can state unequivocally that in those twenty-five years I have never had a better student." If the letter is written by a Nobel Prize winner, so much the better.

How Does the Law School Admissions Process Work?

Applicants whose LSAT scores and undergraduate grade point averages rank them at the top of the applicant pool are generally admitted automatically.

There are many different elements that an admissions committee may consider when making determinations among applicants who are not automatic admits. Applicants who will be admitted must distinguish themselves from the 3,000 others. Having earned an advanced degree or demonstrated an ability to overcome disadvantages or having a minority affiliation, unusual experiences, or outstanding achievements may provide the needed distinction.

When deciding among applicants with similar academic backgrounds, the admissions committee will be looking for the applicant who can bring something special to the first-year class. Show the committee that you are that student.

In Closing . . .

Applying to law school can be a frustrating, expensive, and nerve-racking undertaking. Careful preparation, common sense, and a realistic attitude should greatly increase your chances of getting into the law school of your choice. You may be surprised to find that getting the information you need, and even getting into law school, isn't as difficult as you thought.

DOUBLE YOUR FUN
Joint Degrees

Leianne S. Crittenden

More and more students who are interested in more than just law are opting for programs that combine law with other graduate studies. Leianne S. Crittenden examines the joint law/business program offered at most universities and explores the benefits of spending an extra year to get an M.B.A. Whether in the practice of law or in the business world beyond, the J.D./M.B.A. combination is hard to beat. Author Crittenden sets out the requirements for getting both of these degrees and describes the high points and low points to expect along the way.

There are many reasons to enter a joint-degree program, some more noble than others. Perhaps you have always thought that law was sort of interesting but also knew you wanted something more. Maybe you seek a broader education or the benefits of two educational approaches. You might be trying to find a job that is a mixture of business and law. Perhaps you want to make sure you'll be employable, no matter what the economic circumstances. Or maybe you just want to impress people at cocktail parties.

Many universities offer graduate programs combining various professional degrees (sort of like alphabet soup). Chances are that you could find a program somewhere combining either law or business with one or more of architecture, journalism, medicine, economics, theology, public affairs, or another of the liberal arts. The most common program, however, is probably the law/business combination, known to law schools as the J.D./M.B.A. (and known to the business schools as the M.B.A./J.D.).

Leianne S. Crittenden earned her J.D./M.B.A. from UCLA in 1981. She has worked in private practice, as in-house counsel, and as an investment banker, and she is currently an associate in the business department at Morrison & Foerster in San Francisco, where she facilitates asset-backed transactions.

The joint J.D./M.B.A. program combines the two years of business school and the three years of law school into four years. Note that the J.D./M.B.A. is a joint *program,* as distinct from a joint *degree:* you end up with two pieces of parchment, one a J.D. and the other an M.B.A. You must attend two separate schools and be able to juggle your schedule to meet the requirements for two separate degrees.

© 1984 by Sam Hurt

Are You Really a Masochist?

Your first decision is whether you are ready for four more years of school—not just college, but big bad graduate professional school. You almost certainly will have to go full-time, as pursuing two degrees will keep you plenty busy. By the way, if you plan to go to law school and have any idea that you might be interested in a second graduate degree, do it now—don't kid yourself that you will be able to pick up another degree later. Despite your best intentions, pursuing graduate studies while you are working like a madman is extremely difficult, and evening programs are offered at only a limited number of schools.

Why would anyone want to go to both law school and business school at the same time? I did it because of the flexibility, educational rewards, and increased expertise it would provide. I was interested in both business and law graduate programs and had difficulty choosing between the two, so I did both. I have never regretted it.

While getting both degrees can be a headache, having both degrees has enormous advantages. Two degrees allow you more flexibility in the job market and provide a wider range of opportunities. If you have always had an interest in one specific area of law, following are some of the ways a business degree might fit into your plans (I have provided business job counterparts, also).

M.B.A. concentration	Law school courses	Business/law job
Finance	Securities, business planning	Investment banking, management consulting, securities attorney
Real estate or finance	Real property, tax law	Real estate developer, syndicator/real estate attorney
Accounting	Tax law	Tax accountant, financial planner, tax attorney, estate planning attorney
Personnel	Labor relations, litigation	Personnel administrator, labor arbitrator, union representative, management/union labor attorney
Marketing	Antitrust, litigation	Marketing, strategic planning, antitrust attorney

The Gains

A lawyer with an M.B.A. has more flexibility to leave law and start a career in business. Given the number of young lawyers who grow tired of life at law firms, planning ahead may make sense. The joint-degree program has traditionally been considered good background for a career at a large law firm with a sophisticated corporate law or antitrust practice. An added benefit is that many law firms give joint-degree program graduates an extra year's credit for determining starting salaries and the number of years before consideration for partnership, much as they do for students who have completed judicial clerkships. Many businesses also will pay more to their M.B.A.'s who also have law degrees.

A business degree is particularly useful for corporate (or in-house) counsel, who participate in their company's business decisions to a much greater extent than outside counsel. As lawyers, they are hired in as fairly senior members of the management team and have ready access to senior management. A business degree obviously helps them understand management's goals and objectives more clearly. The corporations most likely to employ in-house counsel include those in regulated industries—such as banks, utilities, insurance companies, and brokerage houses—and large industrial concerns. Many large corporations employ as many lawyers as the largest law firms. Even though the practice of in-house corporate counsel is necessarily specialized—you will learn a lot about insurance law if you work for an insurance company—large companies have a surprisingly varied menu of projects for their legal staffs.

In addition, the curricula of the programs are to some extent complementary. The analytical skills you learn in business school can be useful in law school, and vice versa. The substance also overlaps. My accounting classes made the tax code much easier to understand—I had an idea of why laws were enacted and of what conduct they were supposed to regulate.

School Selection

How do you go about enrolling in one of these J.D./M.B.A. programs? For one thing, you have to take both the GMAT and the LSAT. Beyond that, there really are no prerequisites for law school. Business schools generally like to see that you have some math, economics, and accounting, but don't worry if you are lacking in any of those areas. You will just have to work harder once you are admitted.

Almost every university with a law school and a business school has a joint program. You have to be admitted separately to both the law and the business schools. Remember that if you don't get into both schools (or if you don't initially apply to both), you can always apply to the second school after you have started your first year.

In choosing the right university, consider carefully the strong and weak points of its business and law schools. Where do students get jobs— or do they get jobs? Do the schools draw students and faculty from around the country and have nationwide reputations and job placement, or are they more local? Are the programs at both schools of comparable quality? A university's law school may graduate dozens of federal court clerks each year, while its business school advertises for applicants on the back of matchbook covers.

Note also that while the teaching approach in most law schools is similar, business schools vary. Some take the textbook and blackboard theoretical approach, while others use the case method, which describes an actual business situation and puts the student in the management decision-making role. Many schools combine both, but in varying degrees.

As you may know, for law schools there is an established pecking order of the ten or twenty "best" schools. That order for business schools is less established, and it also varies from specialty to specialty. Some schools are known for finance, some for marketing, some for economic theory, and some for general management.

Also consider how joint-degree students are treated. Do they get scheduling priority if there are conflicts between the business and law schools? Are the law school and the business school even on the same schedule, or is one on the semester system and the other on a quarter system? Wouldn't you love to have midterms and papers due at business school at the same time that you have law school final exams?

Even if you have chosen carefully, your biggest headache once you have selected a university will be schedule conflicts between the two schools. The first two years are easy, at least in terms of scheduling. You do the first year of one program in its entirety, then the first year of the other program. In the last two years, you condense the remaining year of business school and the remaining two years of law school, essentially by taking fewer electives and having the required courses in each school count as electives in the other.

One entertaining sidelight in going through the two programs is seeing the contrast at one university between two different educational traditions with two very different pedagogical approaches. Law school tends to be more academic, with more emphasis on grades, and teaches you an approach such that you can work well on your own. Business school tends to be more practical, with emphasis on experience, and teaches you skills necessary to work well alone or as part of a team. Some joint-degree program graduates have even noted that business school prepared them better for the practice of law than did law school.

The Pot at the End of the Rainbow

As wonderful as the joint-degree program may sound to you, you should be aware that there are skeptics among potential employers. Some law firms are still taken aback at joint-degree students ("Are they really interested in law? How do I know they won't go into business?"). Some businesspeople also have grown averse to lawyers (also known as "deal killers"), although many others do feel that if you can't beat 'em, have one join you. In any event, be prepared to answer the question, "So, what ever made you want to do a joint-degree program, anyway?"

If you had trouble deciding between business school and law school in the first place, just wait until you face the choice of whether to start in a business job or in law. Whatever you had planned at the outset, three summers' worth of jobs while you were completing the two degrees will have given you plenty of food for thought.

You should be aware that there are very few jobs, particularly at entry level, that truly let you utilize both degrees simultaneously. If a business-person has a legal problem, it usually gets referred to in-house corporate counsel or an outside law firm. If you are the businessperson in that position, your employer probably would want you to refer the question, notwithstanding the fact that you have a law degree. Similarly, law firms, although many of their clients are businesses, are not paid to make their clients' business decisions—only to point out the relative legal risks and rights. Your business clients will not want you second-guessing their business judgment, even (or especially) if you do have an M.B.A.

Most joint program graduates start as lawyers, but a significant minority start in investment banking or other areas of finance. Most graduates don't want to foreclose their law options, and since law firms are geared up to hire people directly out of law school, making a lateral move after three or four years in business can be difficult. You also probably would not want to start a business career and then take the bar exam. On the other hand, if you have a novel idea that combines both degrees, you should go out and find the job that meets your standards. If you take the initiative with a good idea, you will find that many employers are interested in discussing your perspective.

Best of all, there are lots of jobs you can pursue down the road if you have both degrees. Certainly the most attractive feature of the J.D./M.B.A. program is having the flexibility offered by two of the most generally respected graduate professional degrees offered. And if you were already planning to go to law school, you can get all of this from just one extra year of school!

A TALENT FOR TORTS
Is Law for You?

Patti Hulvershorn

You may have all the natural ability necessary to be a successful law student, but do you have the aptitudes necessary to be a happy lawyer? Patti Hulvershorn, a career consultant, gives some insight into what makes for satisfied and unsatisfied lawyers.

Many people consider law school a path to an exciting career that will be financially rewarding and interesting. While law school itself is often fascinating to the would-be lawyer, the actual practice of law is sometimes less so. The midcareer dissatisfaction that lawyers may experience is often the result of unused aptitudes—innate talents that can be developed through training and experience.

Aptitudes can be identified and measured with a series of timed work samples, not to be confused with vocational and career tests that measure interests rather than innate abilities. Different careers use different combinations of aptitudes. Those who encounter career dissatisfaction, especially lawyers, have generally selected a position that fails to use a strong aptitude. This unused or underutilized aptitude is a continual source of dissatisfaction, the proverbial pea under the mattress.

Specialist v. Generalist

The typical aptitude profile for happy lawyers in large law firms is fairly straightforward. They are Specialists, as opposed to Generalists, who score low as extroverts. A satisfied lawyer has good analytical thinking skills, an aptitude for handling masses of detailed paperwork, and a good vocabulary (not a great vocabulary, a good one) and scores low in many other aptitudes.

Patti Hulvershorn is a career consultant who works with Career Testing & Guidance in Alexandria, Virginia.

The Generalist prefers a variety of tasks and cooperative sharing of responsibility. The Specialist prefers an independent role and working with others as an authority rather than a team member. Understanding this difference is one of the first steps in determining how, or whether, one fits into a legal career. By determining which roles fit best, you can avoid the mistake, for example, of opening a private practice when you actually prefer the collegial atmosphere of a team-oriented practice.

For Generalists, there are as many ways to do a task as there are people, and the method used is relatively unimportant as long as it is effective and efficient. Specialists know that there are two approaches to a task—their way and the wrong way. Generalists believe that a compromise is a matter of giving up some of what each person wants in order to reach a consensus. Specialists believe that "as soon as you see it my way, we have reached a compromise." Generalists are interested in a wide variety of things and enjoy days composed of eight or ten unrelated tasks, such as responding to mail, attending a staff meeting, interviewing potential employees, attending a long-range marketing strategy session, and reading a professional journal. Specialists prefer days when they spend many hours on a project that is narrow in scope, such as taking 6 hours to research the relevant factors involved in a merger of two companies. For Generalists, delegating and sharing work is natural; Specialists prefer to control the work and do it their own way rather than giving it to someone else.

The vast majority of lawyers who stay in practice and enjoy it are strong Specialists. They become more expert each year in their own narrow field of expertise. The Generalist often becomes bored after several years and yearns to stretch in totally different directions.

Aptitudes That Help and Hinder

There are two primary legal aptitudes, Classification Ability and Concept Organization. The first is the ability to discover the relationships in a mass of seemingly unrelated data (similar to inductive reasoning). The second is the talent for seeing the proper organization of the data. Law school provides a mountain of data for the budding attorney, together with instruction in the methods for retrieving additional information and applying it to new cases. Classification Ability is necessary for selecting the appropriate diagnosis in any given case; Concept Organization is needed for locating the relevant facts and precedents to bolster the presentation of the case. The goal is to find the best fit between the facts in the client's case and precedent.

Although Classification Ability and Concept Organization are the two basic intellectual aptitudes that make the practice of law rewarding, other factors are equally important in determining overall success and

"He always enjoyed playing devil's advocate."

satisfaction in the field. The law student must read and memorize vast amounts of information in order to pass the courses and, later, the bar exam. The student with high Verbal Memory and Visual Dexterity will find law school much less of a challenge than the student low in these aptitudes. Verbal Memory is simply the ease with which one memorizes basic facts, such as the vocabulary of a foreign language or the dates and events in history. Visual Dexterity, sometimes called Perceptual Speed and Accuracy, is the ability to quickly and easily perceive and process written symbols, such as words and numbers, and demonstrates an ease in handling details. A great deal of legal work boils down to proofreading for small details, and this talent allows the lawyer to be more efficient than nontalented colleagues.

There are several aptitudes that are potential burdens for would-be lawyers because the practice of law does not use them: Spatial Relationships, an ability to mentally manipulate three-dimensional objects; Idea Productivity, which is creativity; and the music-related aptitudes of Rhythm Memory, Pitch Discrimination, and Tonal Memory. Most unhappy lawyers have high scores in one or more of these areas. These unused aptitudes draw their owners to activities that are not part of practicing law. Being a sort of round peg in a square hole can lead to some unhappy and frustrating years that can damage one's self-esteem and personal life.

For example, one unhappy lawyer spent every spare minute renovating his house, a hobby that made primary use of his Spatial Relationships aptitude. It was only in the hobby that he found true satisfaction; the time spent in the office was unfulfilling, boring, and increasingly oppressive. After aptitude testing, this lawyer decided to leave his large law firm and work for a medium-sized construction company. He handled its legal problems while training for a career in project development and management, a career that would use his structural aptitudes. He could have entered this career more directly by majoring in civil engineering. The law degree, while it may prove useful, was an unnecessary and expensive step on this lawyer's eventual career path.

The most troublesome aptitude for the would-be practitioner of law is Idea Productivity, which is "aptitude language" for creativity. It is a measure of the number of ideas that flit through your head in a given period of time. If you have difficulty concentrating on a chapter of history in a text, if you find yourself easily bored, or if your mind drifts off while you are engaged in a routine task such as balancing a checkbook, you may have high Idea Productivity. Law requires attention to detail, the ability to concentrate and focus on the task at hand. While some parts of law have creative outlets, the majority of the lawyer's time is spent in comparatively repetitive pursuits. Those with much Idea Productivity become quickly bored and unhappy.

Certain kinds of practice emphasize a particular aptitude more than others, but even when the "troublesome" aptitudes are useful, their absolute amounts should remain fairly low. For example, tax lawyers are generally more satisfied when they have high Visual Dexterity scores and lower Idea Productivity scores than usually found in the typical lawyer profile. Trial lawyers, on the other hand, need a bit more Idea Productivity, but still not as much as individuals in most other fields. More aptitude for Spatial Relationships is especially useful for attorneys involved in matters that focus on construction, architecture, or patents. Those whose practices rely heavily on assisting individuals and companies engaged in transactions, i.e., buying and selling goods, services, property, or companies, are most effective when they have slightly higher Classification Ability. Those who are Generalists, rather than Specialists, can find happiness as lawyers who act as managers of the departments or organizations in which they work. And attorneys whose practices emphasize investigations, such as prosecutors, district attorneys, and white-collar criminal defense lawyers, can use more Classification Ability and more Idea Productivity.

Before you decide to invest in a legal degree to practice law, think carefully about the tasks that you find most rewarding and most dull. Try to assess your own aptitudes. And if you still want to practice, even though you don't fit the typical lawyer profile, review some of the specific kinds of legal positions discussed in this book. You want to find a good match between a career and your own natural abilities.

ANATOMY OF A LAWYER
Personality and Long-Term Career Satisfaction

Susan J. Bell and Lawrence R. Richard

In addition to your natural aptitudes, your personality can affect your long-term happiness in the legal profession. Susan J. Bell and Lawrence R. Richard, both lawyers and career consultants, tell you how a simple personality assessment tool, the Myers-Briggs Type Indicator, can help guide you through the legal career maze.

You've invested thousands of dollars in an undergraduate education and are about to invest thousands more in three years of law school. Will you feel your investment was a sound one ten years from now?

Stories of dissatisfied lawyers abound. A recent study conducted by the ABA indicates that of lawyers who change jobs every year, 40,000 leave the profession. According to a 1984 study by the Young Lawyers Division, even more report dissatisfaction with their current position and their intention to change jobs within two years.

A simple personality inventory can provide some guidance to help keep you out of the ranks of the statistics. The assessment tool, called the Myers-Briggs Type Indicator (MBTI), describes four basic personality preferences that report where you prefer to expend your energy, how you prefer to acquire new information, and how you make decisions. Now the most widely used personality assessment tool, the MBTI is being

In addition to creating and publishing this book, a perfect project for an ENTJ, Susan J. Bell is certified to administer and report the results of the MBTI and provides career counseling services for lawyers in Washington, D.C. Lawrence R. Richard, J.D., is president of Lawgistics, a consulting firm in Philadelphia that specializes in career counseling and planning for the legal profession. He is completing study for his doctorate in psychology and is conducting research about the MBTI and lawyers' career satisfaction. He practiced law ten long years before he found the perfect match for his ENFP personality in his consulting business.

used to identify correlations between certain personality types and career satisfaction.

The MBTI consists of a series of forced-choice questions that, once scored, report an individual's preferences on four different scales. Like legal terms, the words that describe the traits that compose the four scales are almost like another language; they have specific meanings unlike the words' common meanings.

Extraversion/Introversion

The first scale reports where you focus your energy. Extraverts focus on the outer world of people, places, and events. Introverts focus on the inner world of ideas and understanding. Extraverts, who compose about 75 percent of the population, are energized when they are active in their outer world. They are stimulated by meeting new people, seeing new places, and trying new things. They are the proverbial life of the party. They have never heard of Murphy's Law and rush head-on into new activities, assuming everything will work out.

Introverts, on the other hand, are more cautious when approaching a new endeavor. They prefer a depth of understanding rather than the breadth of interests Extraverts prefer. Because the Introverts' favorite world is the inner world, they frequently are seen as quiet and reserved. Parties exhaust them. They try to edit their thoughts to perfectly express their intended meaning before they say a word. As a consequence, they often have little to say at meetings but may have the most meaningful comments to make. Introverts need more time to ponder a response to a new idea or question than Extraverts, who are more likely to talk now and think later.

As lawyers, Introverts have the natural ability to concentrate for long periods of time on single projects and adjust more readily to practices that require much research and thought. Introverts may adapt more easily to the early years of practice in big firms, where spending two weeks in the library researching and writing a single memo is not uncommon. Extraverts, on the other hand, may chafe against such solitary assignments. Their natural outgoing personality often assists them in making contacts and developing clients as their legal experience matures.

Sensing/Intuition

The second scale of the MBTI reports how individuals gather information. People who have a preference for Sensing collect information through their five senses. They trust what they can see, taste, hear, feel, and smell. They have a natural facility with facts and detail. They naturally focus on the present moment and are practical and realistic. They approach tasks in a step-by-step fashion and are very exact. The answer to the question "What time is it?" has only one answer, the hour and minute, for someone who prefers Sensing.

For those who prefer to gather information through Intuition, time is a relative matter. Any time from 10:50 a.m. to 11:10 a.m. can be classified as about 11 a.m. Intuitives collect information through their sixth sense. This does not mean that they are psychic, it means only that they prefer to collect information by focusing on the meanings and understandings behind the raw data with which they are presented. Intuitives' natural home is the future, and they are more comfortable imagining the possibilities than coping with current reality. They rely on their verbal fluency and are often known as wordsmiths. While your Sensing friends may tell you every word of a conversation they had, your Intuitive friends tell you what that conversation really meant.

A natural preference for Sensing can be a great asset to lawyers whose work involves primarily remembering large volumes of facts. This preference can be especially useful to trial lawyers. Current research also indicates that many judges prefer Sensing. Lawyers who prefer using their Intuition naturally keep their eyes on the big picture of their projects. They often have a constant stream of new ideas that can result in constant changes for those who work with them. Intuitives' fountain of ideas can also create novel theories of law to solve their clients' problems.

Thinking/Feeling

Once you have collected information, you can use it to make decisions. The decision-making process is represented by the third scale of the MBTI. Of all the scales, this is the one whose names are least descriptive of the actual processes. Both processes represent rational, valid decision-making methods. Both involve thought, and neither process is related to emotions. The two processes are Thinking and Feeling.

Those who prefer to make decisions on the basis of Thinking prefer to come to closure in a logical, orderly manner. They can readily discern inaccuracies and are often critical. They can easily hurt others' feelings without knowing it. They are excellent problem solvers. They review the cause and effect of potential actions before deciding. Thinkers are often accused of being cold and somewhat calculating because their decisions do not reflect their own personal values. They focus on discovering truth, and they seek justice.

Those who prefer to make decisions on the basis of Feeling apply their own personal values to make choices. They seek harmony and, therefore, are sensitive to the effect of their decisions on others. They need, and are adept at giving, praise. They are interested in the person behind the idea or the job. They seek to do what is right for themselves and other people and are interested in mercy.

Judging/Perceiving

The last scale of the MBTI reflects an individual's life-style. Those who prefer Judging like to live life in a planned, orderly way. Those who prefer Perceiving would rather live life in a flexible, spontaneous, adaptable way. This is probably the easiest preference to spot among your friends and colleagues.

People who prefer Judging like lists, make lists, stick to their lists, and check off the items completed on their lists. They enjoy schedules, and they celebrate endings. They like closure, order, and organization. They may decide too quickly with incomplete information or may not review a decision even when there is new, important information available. At the extreme, those who prefer Judging are sometimes said to have already made up their minds and don't want to be confused by the facts.

Those who prefer Perceiving, in contrast, are quite distractable and at the extreme can get lost between the house and the car. They make lists but rarely carry them out and usually lose them. They are always looking for additional information before they make a decision and, as a consequence, are frequently finishing projects at the last minute. They are chronic users of the all-nighter system. Their openness and curiosity make adapting to new situations and taking advantage of new opportunities second nature.

What It All Means

These attributes combine to provide a four-letter type using the following designations.

E Extraversion		I Introversion	
S Sensing		N Intuition	
T Thinking		F Feeling	
J Judging		P Perceiving	

For example, a person whose type is reported as ENFJ prefers Extraversion, Intuition, Feeling, and Judging.

Certain types seem to appear more often in the legal profession than others. A study conducted in the mid-1960s among law students indicates that NTs and TJs (those who prefer Intuition and Thinking or Thinking and Judging) are most often attracted to law as a career. Six types, each including one of those combinations, accounted for about two thirds of the law students studied. Those types are ISTJ, INTJ, INTP, ENTP, ENTJ, and ESTJ. Those who enjoy abstract theory and problem solving (NTs) and the tough-minded decision makers (TJs) seem naturally attracted to the profession. The only attribute unrepresented in the common lawyer types is Feeling, and this may be the personality characteristic most likely to cause dissatisfaction once the lawyer has entered practice.

© 1989 by Michael Goodman

"I like you, Hardiman . . . that killer instinct so fundamental to the practice of law comes naturally to you."

Being a type different from those appearing in the mainstream of lawyers should not discourage you from practice if you are sure that law is the career you want to pursue. Knowing that you are somewhat out of the mainstream, however, can help you deal more effectively with those types you will encounter most often. As a type not frequently found in a particular career, you may have a unique contribution to make, but you may be swimming upstream in order to make it. That should not discourage you but should only help make you aware of some of the challenges you may encounter along the way.

SWAPPING HORSES IN THE MIDDLE OF A DREAM
Alternative Careers with a J.D.

Dr. Abbie Willard Thorner

You have given careful thought to your own abilities and desires, have studied this book, and are convinced that law is for you. You're off to apply to law school! What if you change your mind about the legal profession after all? Dr. Abbie Willard Thorner, past chair of the National Association for Law Placement, provides ideas on other ways to use your legal skills.

You have carefully read this book and have decided law school is for you. You still wonder, however, what else you might do with your legal degree besides practice law. Stories about lawyers turned medical doctors, playwrights, or ice cream entrepreneurs abound, but these isolated anecdotes are not typical examples of the vast majority of lawyers who move out of the established bounds of practice. There are entirely different disciplines in which legal training is clearly an asset. But there are not ten easy steps to retool a law degree.

The process of becoming a lawyer really involves the shaping of many skills. Some of these are clearly associated with the actual practice of law and include skills in oral advocacy, written argument, and negotiation. Others are much more general and therefore applicable to many disciplines. These include analysis, communication, discipline, thoroughness, and attention to detail.

Law school itself is the process of helping you develop this range of skills. As such, it is an academic means to a practical end. So diverse are these skills and their applicability so broad that a lawyer really fulfills

Dr. Abbie Willard Thorner is Assistant Dean of Placement at the Georgetown University Law Center in Washington, D.C., and was the 1986–87 President of the National Association for Law Placement. She is coauthor of Managing the Recruitment Process, the definitive text on lawyer recruitment, and is the editor of Now Hiring: Government Jobs for Lawyers, published by the ABA Press.

many roles rather than just the one usually designated "attorney." Louis Schwartz, professor of law at the University of California's Hastings College of Law, has summarized these various functions:

> The lawyer is a planner, a negotiator, a peacemaker. Despite the popular stereotype of the lawyer as contentious adversary, the peaceful ordering of human relations overwhelmingly predominates in his or her activities. In the drafting of commercial and labor contracts, treaties, wills, and constitutions, he or she is concerned with achieving orderly arrangements and with avoiding or settling controversy. This requires imaginative anticipation of contingencies, changes of fortune, tragedies, betrayals, and social change.

> The lawyer is a counselor, advising individuals in their varied and complex relationships with one another and the state. Similarly, the lawyer advises groups, corporations, unions, ethnic communities, cities, states, federal departments and agencies, and international organizations. In giving advice, he or she brings into play the lawyer's specialized understanding of the formal structure of society and law as an instrument of social control and betterment.

> The lawyer is an advocate, representing the views, needs, and aspirations of others more effectively than they, uncounseled, could do by themselves.

> The lawyer is a defender of the rights of the individual against the conformist pressures of society.

> The lawyer is an architect of social structure, responding creatively to the needs of a rapidly changing society.

> The lawyer is a social scientist, drawing upon economics, history, sociology, psychology, political science, and anthropology to deal with the problems of individuals, organizations, and communities.

> The lawyer is an educator, especially a self-educator. The process of educating a lawyer never ends. In every controversy he or she must refresh expertise or acquire expertise in a new factual domain.

> The lawyer is a humanist. To study law is to look through the greatest window on life. Here one sees the passions, the frailties, the aspirations, the baseness and nobility of the human condition.

> The lawyer is a leader. All other qualifications converge in thrusting upon the lawyer leadership and responsibility in community life.

Certainly, all of the skills necessary for these roles are not developed in a mere three years of law school. The skills, attitudes, and intellect that got you to and through undergraduate school are important assets in refining your abilities while in law school. What law school will add to your own lifelong process of skills development, however, is a method of thinking and approaching facts or problems in a way different from your friends who do not attend law school.

This newly learned method of problem solving will allow you to construct more orderly arrangements of ideas as you become a better architect of intellectual structures. It will also enable you to think more broadly about alternative perspectives and outcome, which in turn may make you a better planner. Finally, the oral practice with this problem-solving method will facilitate your functioning as an advocate for yourself, others, or causes in which you believe. While these skills better enable you to fulfill the many roles of a lawyer, they also broaden your base of skills for disciplines outside the practice of law.

A recent study conducted by the Harvard Law School Program on the Legal Profession in conjunction with a group of seven northeastern law schools attempted to analyze the career patterns of law school graduates both within and outside of traditional practice. This Career Path Study confirmed what law teachers, prelaw advisers, and parents have been saying for years: law can lead to a range of careers, many of which do not fall under the rubric of traditional law practice but are law-related or nonlegal. Of the respondents to the Career Path Study, from law school classes spanning twenty-two years, only 79 percent were in traditional law practice positions with private law firms, government bodies, public service organizations, and legal departments in business, industrial, educational, and financial institutions. Eight percent were in law-related positions and the remaining 13 percent in positions unrelated to law. In short, more than 20 percent of those individuals trained to be lawyers have chosen not to be lawyers. Why?

The American Bar Association, several state bars, and numerous law school placement offices have attempted to answer this question. While the responses differ depending on who has surveyed whom and when, several generalizations have emerged. Lawyers who choose not to practice law do so for a host of reasons, all of which may be reduced to issues of job satisfaction or self-concept. The most frequently cited reasons for leaving the law include these:

- Traditional law is employment that does not utilize the range of skills developed by an individual in twenty-four-plus years of life and education.

- Salaries offered in such employment, for most lawyers, are not proportional to the quantity of work expected and the amount of time required to produce it.

147

- The limited utilization of skills and the extraordinarily high expectations for amount of work produced both contribute to a work environment characterized by a lack of intellectual stimulation and an abundance of tedium interspersed with excessive pressure.
- Law is a jealous master or mistress and allows no time for other interests or relationships.

Yet many lawyers not only continue to practice law throughout their careers, but also report significant satisfaction with their chosen line of work and its various economic as well as psychological payoffs. What then separates those who like the traditional practice of law from those who leave it? The answers are as varied as the individuals who make the decisions, but in almost every case life-style seems to be a determining variable. If you want to consider carefully your career choice inside as well as outside of traditional practice, you will want to ask yourself several difficult life-style questions:

What is most important to me—work or leisure?

How do I want to apportion the hours in my day?

What standard of living do I need or want to maintain?

What job-related activities do I find most satisfying?

What skills do I have that I want to use or develop?

What types of relationships do I want to foster—friends, family, professional?

What characteristics of a job, its duties, or its environment are important to me?

The answers to these questions will to a great extent determine what jobs and ultimately which career you will want to pursue.

The Career Path Study mentioned earlier also revealed that the longer attorneys were out of law school, the more likely they were to move from law to law-related or nonlegal positions. This dispels the notion that those who pursue alternatives to traditional practice do so because they overreact to a bad law school experience, go through a late adolescent crisis, or cannot find a traditional legal job. It also indicates that such life-style decisions may be made at any time in your career.

If the answers to the questions above take you beyond the life-style associated with traditional law practice, then you will want to read on about the alternatives available to you, which fall into two categories: law-related and nonlegal.

Law-Related Alternatives

Alternative careers related to law allow you to use the skills you have developed in law school while enabling you to expand your law-related duties into broader areas of responsibility. Such jobs are easier to find than nonlegal positions because the circle of contacts developed in the traditional law world may also be helpful in these related areas. Law-related jobs may also be easier to obtain because your skills are more directly transferable, and marketing your experience will therefore be easier. Finally, such jobs, unlike nonlegal jobs, may permit you to return more easily to law later.

The Career Path Study identifies the most common law-related positions, listed below. The brief comments on each provided here are intended to give you a sense of how accessible and desirable such a position might be to you.

Judges. There are three ways to become one—appointment, election, or promotion. Being appointed usually requires a distinguished career and/or a well-placed mentor or political friend. Being elected requires even more political connections. Being promoted into the position of administrative law judge almost always requires former government service.

Law Teachers. The highest level of job satisfaction for lawyers in traditional or law-related positions is reported by law teachers. A good academic foundation with some publishing, practice experience, and maybe even a judicial clerkship all are desirable. Courses to be taught range from traditional law disciplines and legal interdisciplinary law to history, political science, or literature in undergraduate institutions.

Court and Law Firm Administrators. Many law-related organizations now employ individuals to help run or administer their work. Such organizations include bar associations, their sections and committees, and courts at the local, state, and federal levels. Educational institutions (including law schools) and businesses (including larger law firms) also hire individuals who have a law degree or demonstrated experience or education in administration or management.

Mediators. Positions in mediation, arbitration, and labor relations counseling all rely heavily on knowledge of labor law and personnel management. Such positions may be found in settings as varied as national organizations, unions, large corporations, and individual home-based consulting outfits. Many individuals who have been successful in this cluster of alternatives have apprenticed themselves in a mentor or guild type of relationship to someone already established in the field.

Law Librarians. Law librarians not only serve law schools, but may also be found in courts, government agencies, corporate legal departments, bar associations, and private firms. A master's degree in library science is almost always required, with a law degree frequently desired. As computers and technology have become increasingly important in library holdings and services, so has this type of technological expertise become valued in applicants for these positions.

Law Enforcement Officials. While law enforcement has traditionally been associated with local police forces, alternatives have multiplied as such police forces have become more sophisticated in their services and as law enforcement itself has become more broadly defined. The FBI and CIA offer national and international examples, while positions as hearing officers in state and local agencies or human relations specialists provide other options. Some law enforcement training or experience as well as course work in criminal law or criminology is helpful.

Government Contract Officers. Government agencies at the federal, state, and local levels purchase goods and services. Experience in such procurement and an understanding of and interest in contracts are helpful for public- and private-sector employment in this area.

Legal Consultants. Consultants, broadly defined, are individuals whose experience and expertise allow them to sell what they know. Law firms and government agencies use consultants to advise them on personnel, training, management, marketing, computer, finance, and client development issues, among others. Extensive experience in one of these areas and high visibility among contacts in firms or agencies seem to be most important for this alternative.

Legal Trainers. Many state and local bar associations, as well as law schools and for-profit continuing legal education entities, now conduct seminars and training programs for lawyers. A law degree and some background in educational program design are helpful.

Lobbyists. Frequently employed by trade associations, special interest groups, and consulting firms, lobbyists attempt to influence lawmakers. They may work at the federal or state level and may be involved in a variety of activities, ranging from government affairs to administrative rule making, legislative drafting, and regulatory reform. Experience with a legislative body is helpful. So too is expertise in one or more substantive areas (such as energy, taxation, or foreign affairs) that might be covered by the legislative process.

Nonlegal Alternatives

Nonlegal alternatives available to law graduates differ from law-related alternatives in several important ways. A law background—both educational and experiential—may or may not help, depending on the discipline. Because of this, you may encounter more difficulty in identifying and then finding a job. You will probably experience similar difficulty in marketing yourself and convincing an employer of your value for any position. Some job seekers in pursuit of nonlegal jobs have even reported that they encountered an overt bias against applicants with prior legal experience. Some interviewers, rightly or wrongly, believe that those individuals trained in law will have neither the interest in nor the skills for tasks that are not in some way law-related.

While this attitude is a formidable impediment to your search, it pales in comparison to your own attitudes about the value of a law job versus one that is nonlegal. Psychologically, one of the most potentially damaging aspects of a nonlegal job search is your own sense that you are settling for something less prestigious and less financially promising than a traditional law position. Many individuals in search of nonlegal alternatives see themselves as second-class citizens and, unfortunately, communicate this self-concept in their interviews.

While neither your own nor the interviewer's attitudes about a nonlegal job search are insurmountable hurdles, they are nevertheless important constraints for which you will want to be prepared. You will want to explore by yourself and with the help of a career counselor the background, attitudes, and skills that might lead you to a nonlegal job by way of law school. The education you obtained prior to or after law school will be important, as will any employment experience you have had outside of a traditional legal setting. You will also want to consider whether you are willing to explore alternatives that require either more education or some period of on-the-job training. Both may require an ability and willingness on your part to accept a life-style based at least temporarily on less financial reward.

Nonlegal alternatives that seem most appropriate for individuals with law backgrounds fall into three primary clusters: business, service, and independent. There are actually no purely business, service, or independent jobs, only those that seem to emphasize one set of skills more than—but not to the exclusion of—others.

Business

All businesses are involved in trade or commerce of some type. The range of goods and services to be bought or sold is as broad as our Western culture, but you will probably want to focus your search on the corporate, accounting, manufacturing, or entrepreneurial segments of this broad business cluster.

The corporate world is one of the most appealing to those with legal training because within the corporate setting, lawyers can move both into and out of the corporate legal department and management hierarchy with relative ease. Good upward mobility exists outside of the legal department and includes executive, general management, personnel, marketing, public relations, communications, and planning positions.

Accounting firms, frequently considered part of the corporate world, have in recent years expanded far beyond a mere accounting function to provide a range of business services. These include fields as diverse as tax auditing, estate planning, financial management, personnel services, research, training and development, and consulting in areas such as communications, marketing, and technology.

The third category in this business cluster, manufacturing, is concerned with the production of, as well as the transfer of, goods and services. An undergraduate degree and some work experience in a related area are useful in jobs in the most active manufacturing areas: high technology, chemicals, food production, pharmaceutical and medical products, textiles, office equipment, and utilities.

The fourth and final category in this cluster, the entrepreneurial, usually attracts individuals who like to organize and manage a business with some risk but potential gain in its future. Real estate development and capital investment management are the most obvious choices in this category. If you're a risk taker, starting and owning your own business may be another alternative.

© 1985 by Sam Hurt

Service

Unlike the business cluster, the service cluster is characterized more by an interest in performing work for other people than by interest in the goods or rewards produced. The services world certainly has its business interests, but these are combined with, or secondary to, providing a service.

The most businesslike area in the service industry is a group of institutions offering financial services. These include commercial banking, investment banking, financial planning, and stocks or commodities trading. Also included here is the insurance industry, in which a variety of opportunities exist in sales and as an adjuster, claims analyst, title examiner, or financial and estate planner.

The second field in this cluster, government, is very broad and provides opportunities at the local, state, and federal levels. City management, urban planning, and legislative support, as well as the more obvious civil service positions, are just a few examples of the variety of alternatives. And this variety is not limited by geography. Not only do such positions exist in every town and city in the country, but foreign service positions are also available, with appropriate training and experience, around the world.

An arm of the government, law enforcement, is the third area in the service cluster. Like their law-related counterparts, nonlegal positions can be found at the federal, state, and local levels. They range from FBI and CIA agents at the national and international levels to state probation officers and legislative committee aides at the state level, to human resource specialists and advisers in local mayoral offices.

The most obvious segment of the service cluster is the one concerned with individual welfare, including organizations involved in public education and health care. Teachers, trainers, educational and health-care administrators, and school and hospital board members are but a few of the options that lawyers have chosen as they have moved out of traditional practice.

Independent

The independent cluster, while providing services to certain segments of the population, is a cluster in which you will find the opportunity to work independently and autonomously. The three areas in which lawyers have found the most opportunities for this going-it-alone approach to work include personal services, communications, and consulting.

Personal services are provided by individuals as diverse as agents to sports or entertainment figures and counselors in the fields of financial, estate, or tax planning; stress management; and career planning. Executive search firms and outplacement firms (those that counsel and provide support to individuals who have been fired or laid off) also number among their employees many former practicing attorneys.

Communications work is a less obvious and less financially promising option, but it may be for you if you find autonomy to be an important aspect of your work. Free-lance writing and editing for legal publications provide extraordinary freedom but may also inspire extraordinary uncertainty in the number and types of assignments and the resulting compensation. The publishing industry, especially the segment that produces law school texts or law-related newsletters, also attempts to attract individuals with law training.

Consulting, of which communications work is frequently a part, provides a broader array of job alternatives if you have expertise to offer in fields such as marketing, personnel management, financial planning, business development, professional training, or office technology. The uncertainty of remuneration coupled with the going-it-alone characteristic of most of the personal services options make this one, as well as the others, satisfying primarily to the more independent risk takers among us. Having contacts in the market you hope to serve is also a prerequisite to setting up your own consulting business.

The options are many, but so too are the trade-offs, many of which require your personal decisions about financial security, life-style, and self-concept. Recent years have found legal practice becoming even more specialized and legal education ever more expensive. Because of this, law is no longer an economical generalist education that opens any and all doors. It is, however, a respected profession in which career movement both within and outside of its bounds is increasing rapidly. For individuals who choose law as a means to an end rather than a career in itself, the skills associated with law school and lawyering—analysis, communications, discipline, thoroughness, and attention to detail—will serve them and their careers well.

PERSPECTIVES ON BEING A LAWYER

DIRECTED VERDICT
Closing the Book on
My Legal Career

Brett M. Campbell

Brett M. Campbell decided to end his legal career during its infancy. With humor and insight, he explains why and provides food for thought for those who have not yet taken the plunge.

Spring semester, third year. Everyone's bored with law school and ready to get out. The conversation turns from classes and interviews to new jobs, new cities, new lives. I'm no exception; I have a real prize to look forward to—a yearlong judicial clerkship. And after that . . .

After that, I just don't know. I'm supposed to be thinking about what law firms I'll interview with next year, but I'm not looking forward to picking a firm, a city, or a specialty. In fact, the more I think about it, the feeling is undeniable: I don't want to practice law at all.

It was time to rethink my career choice, before I had too much of an investment in the lawyer life-style. Why had I chosen that path in the first place? In looking back, I realized I hadn't really *made* the decision to become a lawyer. It just sort of . . . happened.

It happened because I'd gotten caught in The System, the stream where society spawns its paper warriors. Like fish in a salmon ladder, the bright and talented are funneled into the money-centered professions, driven by the force of society's need for lawyers, investment bankers, and corporate functionaries. For me, the steps included high school debate champ, college honors program, extracurricular jock, and law student. It seemed so natural a progression that, at my first law school party, I wasn't surprised to find myself in a circle of about ten former debaters

Brett M. Campbell ended his legal career after his judicial clerkship. He works as a journalist and free-lance writer in Austin, Texas.

and politicos. When you surround yourself with others who share your mind-set, it's easy to flow along with the current.

Once you arrive in a highly rated law school, you're channeled toward a Big Firm, big-bucks practice. The mechanical interview process brings high-profile firms right to your door. Expensive lunches, first-class flights to the home office, and, of course, starting (starting!) salaries approaching $65,000 soon follow. Classes and journals, the books of scholarly articles written by professors and students and edited and produced by a select group of the law school's students, gobble any free time or energy that would permit you to consider alternatives to "the jealous mistress." Finally, school debts, grade competition, peer pressure—all combine to erode even the sturdiest resistance to big-firm pressure. You can almost see the shame radiating from the few unfortunate third-years who don't have offers yet.

Understand, I'm not saying law school is a total waste; in fact, I'd sign up again. You learn a lot about how the world really runs, not least by picking up the vocabulary of policy and power. For fuzzy-minded idealists like me, it's a bracing splash of reality. Law school teaches rigorous analytical skills that are useful in almost any field: quite simply, I learned how to think better. It also gives you the credibility that goes with a respected credential—and deservedly so; law school is a giant pencil sharpener that really does sharpen the minds of those pushed into it, even as it reduces and narrows them.

© 1985 by Sam Hurt

But what about what follows? Practicing law certainly has its attractions. It rewards ingenuity, skillful reasoning, and often writing (albeit of a dull and desiccated kind). Lawyers have greater flexibility than most workers; if you don't like your supervising partner, you can go hang out your own shingle, assuming you're prepared to work 80-hour weeks for a few years. Plus, a law degree is a safety net that will catch you if you fail at, say, a business venture or political race. Besides these material benefits, law (unlike most other professions) offers the opportunity to right

wrongs, to "do good"—although too many leave law school having settled for doing well.

Then why did I bail out? Why did a judge I know remark, "Law is the
only profession that everyone's working to get out of"?

Boredom is a big part of it. Law is so procedure and detail oriented
that most day-to-day work is terminally tedious. Plodding through corporate documents, answering interrogatories, poring over countless
cases—it's pretty grim going most of the time. After you've learned the
ropes, much of what you do in your ensuing career grows routine. But
that doesn't stop it from being life consuming. The young lawyers who
earn those princely salaries work hours better suited to slaves—usually
70 hours a week for young big-firm associates on partnership track.

Stress is the other great liability. The really exciting kinds of law—especially litigation—are fraught with deadlines, time pressure, and high
stakes for your clients. The courtroom battle itself, where a missed or late
objection can cost a client millions, is nerve-racking enough. But first
come months of grunge work that must nevertheless be performed accurately, as the trial date looms closer and closer. Then, often as not, the
case—though not your stomach—settles "on the courthouse steps."

The truth is that if you want even marginally interesting work or po-
tent paychecks, you've got to pay with long hours away from family and
friends and a sour stomach. That's why almost all my friends who've just
hatched into fledgling lawyers never chirp with enthusiasm. The best
they can manage are those strained smiles. They are always tired.

Drawbacks all, to be sure, but many jobs share them—without sharing
the considerable rewards. A good lawyer in a major metropolitan area
can make $80,000 after only five years, and with that kind of money, it's
easy to start playing when you're through practicing. That's enough to
keep a lot of otherwise-inclined attorneys slogging through briefs and
pleadings for years after the other layers of gloss have rubbed off.

But it wasn't enough for me. Once the novelty of learning to "think
like a lawyer" wore off, once my friends reported (or betrayed) their
disappointment, once I emerged from school and saw what I'd actually
be doing hour after billable hour, year after pinstriped year, it hit me:

I just didn't care.

When you practice law, you work for someone else—your clients. You
do what's important to *them*. It's true that public interest work can give
you the feeling that you're really accomplishing something important;
at least you're doing something that matters to more than a company
accountant. But even there, the lawyer's actual daily duties (legal research, reading records) are excruciatingly dull, to me anyway. At most,
legal work can occasionally engage you in the same way a crossword puz-
zle or detective novel can. Sure, it beats flipping hamburgers or digging
ditches, but all that ingenuity, all that brainpower—it all goes into

clever, but emotionally sterile, intellectual manipulations. In sum, the work itself—as opposed to what it sometimes produces—is seldom *self*-fulfilling.

But so what? How many jobs do bring meaning to life? Very few. But there's no escaping it—when I look down the road and think about how my obituary will read, I want it to say more than just "lawyer." I want to look back on a life I cared about. And I don't care about law. It's that simple.

Fortunately, I see an alternative: writing. Even when I was clerking for law firms, I enjoyed crafting legal memos more than winning the lawsuit that prompted them in the first place. I want to write (journalism first, then on to other nonfiction and maybe even fiction eventually) because I want to pour my energy into vessels that exercise and reward the creativity, authenticity, and self-expression that I find so vital to my fulfillment—but can't find enough of in the law. Now that my judicial clerkship has ended, I hope to spend my life learning about, and writing about, things that really mean something to me. Shortly after making this decision, I found I wasn't alone.

About an hour after I graduated, I flew to see friends in Los Angeles. We attended a studio screening of the recent Richard Attenborough movie, *Cry Freedom*. In it, Kevin Kline, who plays the courageous South African newspaper publisher Donald Woods, mentions that one of his old law profs would be defending him against the government's trumped-up charges. Had he been a law student? I wondered.

As I complimented the director (who was there to get feedback from the audience), he pointed me toward a rather distinguished-looking fellow in a tweed jacket. It was Donald Woods, there to see his story. Yes, he'd been to law school (which had, incidentally, taught him to hate apartheid; the system was irreconcilable with the principles of justice he studied there). But when he started practicing, "Instead of crusading for justice, I found myself spending all day writing letters demanding money from various people for my clients," he told me.

In his spare time, though, he wrote other letters—letters to the newspaper, letters about things important to him. "One day, someone from the paper called and asked if I wanted to write about public affairs full-time—at half my law salary," he remembered. "I jumped for it." He soon became a foreign correspondent, editor, and, almost reluctantly, crusader for justice. Then an exile, and not a wealthy one. Any regrets, I asked?

"I hadn't been at it [journalism] 5 minutes when I knew I'd made the right decision," he said, "and I've never looked back."

I'm not either. Instead, I'm looking at the road ahead. And for the first time in a long time, I like what I see.

IS IT WORTH THE CLIMB?
The View from the Top

James Upchurch III

James Upchurch III, a Harvard Law School graduate who practiced for several years in Montgomery, Alabama, made it to the top only to rethink whether the view was worth the climb. In this no-nonsense, highly personal account of that climb and his reasons for quitting law to edit a weekly city magazine, Upchurch talks candidly about his own rules to follow in considering law firm practice.

After eleven years of practicing law in a prestigious firm in a good-size southern city, I quit. Quit the firm. Quit practicing law. I stopped climbing—took a deep breath and without looking backward or forward asked myself, "Is the view from the top really worth the climb?"

That was two years ago. I now write for, edit, and co-own a little city magazine in a city that everybody thought was too small to support such a publication. I don't get paid much, and neither does anybody else associated with the publication. I don't often wear a power suit these days, and some seem confused about how to deal with me, as they never did when I was introduced as a lawyer. That can sometimes be uncomfortable.

"Quitting," or changing the road markings in my climb toward big-time partner, involved choices and living with the consequences of those choices. A Harvard law degree is a gold star not easily earned; quitting law practice meant rethinking about those three years of challenging, sometimes grueling study.

And then there was that old greenback dollar staring me in the face. The money from law practice with a well-respected firm is a sizable gold carrot. As partner in a defense and corporate firm, my income was strong incentive to keep mustering the stairs. For most lawyers, practice with

James Upchurch III graduated from Harvard Law School in 1975 and practiced until 1985 with a twenty-attorney firm in Montgomery, Alabama. He is now editor of Montgomery! *magazine, a weekly city magazine published in Montgomery.*

similar firms generates a sufficient income—as long as they don't have a Donald Trump complex.

And in many ways, I was well cut out to practice law. Bright, strong analytical mind, persuasive speaker—I fit the corporate/trial lawyer mold. When I wanted to practice law, I was actually quite good at it. I just realized consciously after about ten years, and unconsciously long before that, that I didn't want to do it often enough, or deeply enough. At least not enough to pay the rising price of succeeding in law practice.

If you have any sense at all, you already know that practicing law can be a little like running that proverbial gauntlet. And if you are a certain kind of person, you won't care. At least not enough to quit. You will be able to view what you give up and endure (long hours of dull reading, deadlines, eyes popping open at 3 a.m. the night before a trial—the sign of your subconscious mind running round and round in what a former partner calls "the squirrel cage"—leaving your family in Florida to endure five boring days in a smoke-filled conference room in North Dakota punctuated by greasy lunches with arrogant, overweight businessmen who think you *are* the American legal system that caused all their problems, etc.) as the Price of a Successful Law Practice. But if you are another kind of person, it will eventually get to you, one way or the other. It's just a matter of time.

Admittedly, my experience is limited. I practiced with one defense firm of a certain size, in a certain place, with particular people. So take my advice with a grain of salt, please. But I do suggest that what I know now, and wish I had known fifteen or twenty years ago, may be of use to you even if you are looking at law practice with another firm, in another city. So—such as they are, here are my Rules to Follow in Considering Law Firm Practice.

Be Sure You Are Chasing What You Want

If you are getting ready to practice law because you admire Atticus Finch, the hero of Harper Lee's great novel *To Kill a Mockingbird,* think again. Rare is the opportunity to play Atticus in the modern-day courtroom drama. Most of your time will not be spent in the courageous defense of the world's Tom Robinsons.

Not that defense-firm clients are devils in disguise. I never represented anybody I thought was evil (I was lucky!), though I did represent a good number who regarded laws (sometimes even of basic safety awareness) as subversive inconveniences to be ignored. As a litigation partner in an insurance defense firm, I had to take what came through the door. And no Tom Robinsons ever came, and I didn't have the time or energy to go after them. I put in my dues with the local indigent defense program and met a double handful of clients who were frequently demanding and ignorant about the basic rules of life. Somewhere deep down, I thought that out of gratitude these people would bring me baskets of turnip greens or tied-up chickens like clients left outside Atticus Finch's door. But they didn't. Payment of the huge bills (the economics of law-firm practice forced me to send to my clients) was sufficient to satisfy any lingering urge they might have had to express their thanks. Many of my clients were insurance companies that tend to fall short in the "Thanks, Jim" department.

I am not complaining. My expectations were unrealistic, that's all. The point is that you have to have a realistic view of why you want to practice law, so that the gentleman or lady lawyer you see in the mirror each morning will have some relation to that projected self-image that got you into law practice in the first place ten or twenty years ago. Before you go to work for a firm—or anywhere in the law, I suppose—write yourself a little essay that describes what your professional and personal life will be like in ten years. Be specific: How will you spend your evenings and weekends? What will your relationship be with your clients? When will you go to work, and when will you go home?

Then inquire, and keep your eyes and ears open, about life at the place where you want to practice. If the daily schedule and the client profile and the demands of the life seem to correspond to your honest mental picture, then you are on the right path. If the correspondence is not there—and remember, no wishful thinking—hesitate. Think carefully. You are probably headed for a great deal of heartache, and it will not be worth it no matter what you earn. You only have one life, and enough jarred expectations will conspire to make you unhappy that you don't need to inflict such a burden on yourself.

Listen to Your Inner Self—And Pay Attention

I had a rather interesting experience with my law firm. It changed while I was there, reflecting changes in top-level personnel through death and retirement, changes in the profession as a whole, and changes within some of the individuals who made up the firm.

When I started as an associate in 1975, the firm was successful—a long-standing practice in a smallish town with a close-knit group of middle-aged partners who were real friends. So were many of the younger associates and partners. There was a sense of shared experience and good will. Hard work came and went; caseloads were shared as work flow bunched up; we had lunch together often and enjoyed swapping stories about our cases and clients. There was a real sense of shared enterprise. The demands were tolerable, and much of the work enjoyable.

Let me make it clear: I liked the people there at the beginning, and I liked the ones who were there at the end. The firm, however, changed. It became more businesslike—a change in management styles and computerization resulted in constant comparison of itemized billings and considerable pressure to maintain and increase one's billable hours. The correlation between influence within the firm and dollars billed became more visible. Rates increased. Income increased. Business boomed.

A sense of competition within the firm became much more intense—or maybe I just became more aware of it, I'm not sure. Everybody's billable hours shot up, on paper and in reality. I would go a month or more without talking shop over lunch with a single partner or associate, without having any fun with them at all. And I liked these people; I felt a real sense of loss that I couldn't identify for a long time. And I was too busy to change the driving pace toward more billable hours, at the expense of friendship within the firm.

From a business point of view, I think many of these changes were for the good and probably overdue. And I don't blame the firm for them; they were largely necessary adaptations to the changing realities of law practice and probably typical of life at a hard-driving, big-city firm. I don't know. But I wish we had all worked harder to keep them from crushing what was an important part of the firm's life.

I would like to have been more aware of what was happening and more aggressive about stopping it—not the efficiencies, but the unintended antisocial consequences of change. And, much earlier in my career, I wish that I had been more sensitive and more willing to act on my own growing feelings of dissatisfaction.

© 1985 by Sam Hurt

I have a good friend who is an architect in Atlanta. He used to change firms every two or three years, and it disconcerted me greatly. We had a long talk about it, and he was just as astonished at my willingness to stay put as I was at his professional portability. I was sure that someday he would be on the street, having already quit every firm in Atlanta. He was equally sure that someday I would regret having stuck in the same rut, as he viewed it, despite being vaguely dissatisfied.

He was right, and I was wrong. I should have done something—moved on; quit; tried another firm, another type of practice, or even another town—much earlier. I might still have eventually quit practicing law, but maybe not. Maybe I would have found a better way to make the career work for me.

Don't be afraid to change if you feel strongly that you have made a mistake or if the firm changes on you. And most of all, be open to those feelings. Don't deny them or just hope they will go away.

Don't Forget Things of the Spirit

Don't stop here; I am an exceedingly unlikely source for a sermon. But don't overlook the fact that practicing law, at a firm or otherwise, means making professional decisions that have moral and spiritual consequences that will be different for each person. You may be able to deal with these choices, but don't think you can avoid them or that you won't care, since it's just a job. It's not just a job. It's a life.

I am not talking about the easy decisions: whether to tear up an incriminating document, encourage a client to lie, or suggest that a potential witness take an extended vacation. I was, and am, proud of my law firm in that respect. The longtime managing partner of the firm took the lead, clearly and absolutely, in ruling out such tactics—not that any of my partners needed much leading in that department. But sometimes an associate needs reminding that winning the case, while important, isn't the only consideration.

I went into law largely on the strength of the common belief that representing the occasional bad guy was all right, because I was going to be an active participant in a larger justice-seeking system in which right was usually vindicated, and the system would only work if I did my job well. Therefore, civilians expressing distaste at the gun-for-hire image of lawyers were simply ill informed.

Well, I wasn't wrong, exactly. In my head, I know that this view is acceptable. But in my heart, it wasn't right for me. I experienced real pain at representing people who seemed dishonest and manipulative. (Let me say that many of my clients were fine, good, and caring people, as yours will be.) But when some of my clients wouldn't live up to their obligations, when the system failed or, as it did sometimes, succeeded for what I thought were the wrong reasons (local favoritism, judicial ignorance, poor preparation by one lawyer or the other), I felt disappointed. Hurt. To argue an untenable position with feigned passion or beat out some injured and needy person became, in time, less and less acceptable, in the same way that winning a big award from a prejudiced and inflamed jury on behalf of some semitruthful malingerer would have cut against my grain. Of course, the complication is that winning is so darned *satisfying,* or so it often seems. So I kept reaching for a brass ring always just beyond my grasp.

The last straw came with a sudden realization in the middle of reciting a favorite law "war story." I was telling with some bravado the tale of how I intimidated a young motel-rape victim out of trying her case into a modest settlement by asking her a string of detailed questions about her colorful sex life. I heard myself reciting the painful degrading of this victim and realized how wide a gulf had grown between the kind of person I wanted to become and the person I was in fact becoming.

Professionally, I wasn't wrong to ask the woman these questions. In her complaint, she had claimed damages for loss of sexual satisfaction; I gave her and her lawyer the opportunity to withdraw those allegations if she didn't want to undergo that line of questioning, and inexplicably—probably on her attorney's advice—she wouldn't. So the questions had to be asked, and they were, and very well too.

But in the middle of retelling that very interesting story one day, I suddenly heard myself telling it. It was funny, but the humor degraded and demeaned another human being. I realized how many of my stories of success at law, true stories within the limits of anecdotal license, were mean in spirit. I judge no one. But for me, the price tag of success became too high to pay.

It would be nice to say I arrived at a successful way to practice trial law without being less than a gentleman, but I couldn't—maybe you can. It would be nice to say that at that moment, I quit practicing law and went into the field of Good Works, but I didn't. To my regret and I am sure to that of my firm, I kept on practicing for about three years after that moment of realization, trying fitfully and unsuccessfully to find a way not to sacrifice what everybody had always told me would be a great career. But the heart had gone out of it.

The point is not that this will also happen to you. Maybe it won't, and if it does, maybe you will deal with the realization of what law practice can be about with greater insight and ease. I hope so. Just don't ignore the risks and the price of the brass ring.

Every lawyer, from the lone dinosaur to the corporate partner, must at some time come to terms with the moral demands of law practice. Representing the "guilty" isn't morally wrong, representing the rich against the poor isn't morally wrong, representing a client you think (deep down) should lose isn't morally wrong—but each involves a moral decision. Lots of good people make those decisions every day and make good lawyers. Just be sure you can.

So—before you take that first step up the stairs, envision the view from the top. Think about what you want and who you are. There are other climbs, perhaps with better views. It's your choice. Climb with conscience and commitment, and remember that there's no better advice to young lawyer or old than "to thine own self be true."

166

NO REGRETS

Judge Thomas P. Jackson

Throughout this book, we have tried to give you an accurate view of the legal profession—warts and all. In this closing piece, Judge Thomas P. Jackson tells you why we are proud to call ourselves lawyers.

Since July 1982, I have been a federal judge in Washington, D.C. Before that, I practiced law as a private lawyer in the local and federal courts of the District of Columbia and the state courts of Maryland.

Being the son of a lawyer, I was exposed to the profession from earliest memory. As a teenager I was alternately attracted and repelled by the idea that I might become a lawyer (as most teenagers are ambivalent about parental example), but the prospect was never far from my mind. One by one, as I matured, I gave up ambitions of professional baseball, deep-sea diving, and journalism. Ultimately, since I respected and admired my father, and observed that he was respected and admired by others, I decided that the law would be my profession too. About midway through college it became clear to me that I had an aptitude for the law, and the law had a deepening fascination for me. Accordingly, following my military service, I entered law school in the fall of 1961.

There were times in law school when, perplexed about what I was supposed to be learning and overwhelmed with the work necessary to learn it, I had misgivings about my choice of career. They passed, and so did I. I was admitted to the bar after passing the bar examination following graduation from law school, and I have never since regretted my choice of careers. Never.

Lawyers practice their craft in a great variety of ways. Some spend their lives forming and merging intricate business enterprises. Others put together complex property transactions. Still others write statutes, or in-

---

Judge Thomas P. Jackson serves on the bench of the United States District Court for the District of Columbia and was formerly a partner in a Washington law firm now known as Jackson & Campbell, P.C. He is a member of the American College of Trial Lawyers and a former chair of the Young Lawyers Section of the Bar Association of the District of Columbia.

surance policies, or estate plans. I was a trial lawyer, meaning, simply, that I represented clients in court. Their causes were mine. If I was successful, they prevailed. If I failed in making clear to a judge or jury that my client's conduct had been lawful, the client suffered the consequences. I succeeded more often than I failed, and, thus, I suppose it could be said I was a successful lawyer. I would agree, but I define my success somewhat differently. To me, my success was found in the skill with which I did my job, win or lose.

First, I would search my client's case for a just position to take. No client is ever totally righteous. Yet none is wholly evil, either. Being an effective advocate for clients is a matter of finding that which is honest and honorable about their situation and then making sure that the judges or juries who must decide their fate are aware of the good they have done and give them maximum credit for it. Having once found the justice in my clients' cause, I never had difficulty with my own conscience being an ardent spokesman for it.

I also resolved that I would never allow myself to submit to a court or jury any effort on a client's behalf of which I was not personally proud. I would never file a pleading or a brief or make an argument that I was not prepared to have all the world know was mine. It would represent the best work of which I was capable at the time. As the years passed, and I won more cases, my confidence in myself grew, because it became apparent to me that my best work was as good as or better than that of others, or I would not be winning.

Finally, I was taught by professional elders to do the honorable and/ or gracious thing whenever I had a choice. Notwithstanding the criticism made of lawyers by the public, which is provoked by the unconscionable conduct of a few to the undeserved disgrace of the remainder, the profession itself is—and has always been—honorable. Its ideals are noble. It demands that its practitioners be people of integrity. And while it may be disappointed in its expectations from time to time, it still strives to bring out the best in those who call themselves lawyers. Consequently, I have always believed that lawyers should never attempt to take unfair advantage of an adversary, using a client's wealth, power, or influence to defeat a just claim. They should never deceive or misrepresent, or deliberately delay justice, or force cases to trial against adversaries who are unprepared through no fault of their own.

I don't mean to congratulate myself for being particularly virtuous. I simply found it easier to be a good lawyer if I truly believed that I was pursuing a just course and had no qualms of conscience. I could, then, speak with conviction when I argued for my client's position. I learned in youth that I was neither an accomplished liar nor a proficient bully. Thus, for very pragmatic reasons, honesty was simply the best policy.

My career, to this point in my life, has been all I could have wished for. I hope there is a good deal more of it yet to come. I have made hundreds of friends, fast and warm friends, among my colleagues at the bar. All of them, to no surprise to me, seem to share my philosophy. We have been vigorous antagonists in court and amiable companions elsewhere. We enjoy one another's respect, our shared experiences in service to our clients and our profession, and a common belief that our efforts have made a positive contribution toward a society in which there is equal justice under law.

© 1988 by Michael Goodman